A LEGION OF STRANGERS

ARTHUR BARLOW

All rights reserved. No part of this book shall be reproduced or transmitted in any form or by any means, electronic, mechanical, magnetic, photographic including photocopying, recording or by any information storage and retrieval system, without prior written permission of the publisher. No patent liability is assumed with respect to the use of the information contained herein. Although every precaution has been taken in the preparation of this book, the publisher and author assume no responsibility for errors or omissions. Neither is any liability assumed for damages resulting from the use of the information contained herein.

Copyright © 2012 by Arthur Barlow

ISBN 978-0-7414-7465-0 Paperback
ISBN 978-0-7414-7466-7 Hardcover
ISBN 978-0-7414-7467-4 eBook

Printed in the United States of America

This is a work of fiction. Names, characters, places, and incidents either are the product of the author's imagination or are used fictitiously. Any resemblance to actual events or locales or persons, living or dead, is entirely coincidental.

Published April 2012

INFINITY PUBLISHING
1094 New DeHaven Street, Suite 100
West Conshohocken, PA 19428-2713
Toll-free (877) BUY BOOK
Local Phone (610) 941-9999
Fax (610) 941-9959
Info@buybooksontheweb.com
www.buybooksontheweb.com

A Legion of Strangers

ONE

The first light of day appeared on the horizon as the sailing vessel 'Mary Cassidy' entered Boston's busy harbor. A lone figure stood on the prow examining the shore. John Reilly, late of the 84th Foot of the British Army, waited patiently for the ship to berth. It would be a new beginning! He was a strong virile man who had seen harsh service in the Army of Britain's foreign wars. His clothing seemed out of place on him and he longed for his uniform and the stripes that had once designated his former rank of Sergeant Major. With large biceps and hammy thighs and well-muscled legs he looked what he was, a battle hardened veteran of the British Army. He had come to America to make a fresh start. Now he was for the golden door as the Irish called America. He crossed the gangplank and leaped onto the quay. He had arrived!

A man in uniform stopped John. He knew not to which service he belonged as he didn't recognize the uniform. The man was an officer of the Immigration and Naturalization Service. The man asked John, "Immigrant?"

When John Reilly said that he was indeed an immigrant the man directed him to a desk where a clerk asked him about himself.

After talking to John for some time the man directed him to a sort of barracks building. "You'll be in quarantine for a week. Then you will be issued papers and released.

John Reilly bided his time with the other immigrants discussing the news of the day. Boston was a hive of activity and the newcomers were anxious to enter the city, to savor their new freedoms. Some simply wished a home they could call their own. Others wanted land for farming. These things were unobtainable in Protestant Ireland.

"They'll even allow you to vote!" One of John's countrymen stated. "And even send your child to school to learn to read and write."

This quieted the Irish who enjoyed no such freedoms in the Old Country as most of them now thought of their former homeland. It had been against the law to teach Irish children and any offender was hauled in front of the assizes where, if found guilty, he was sentenced to death. It was a cruel, hard life. The famine that ravaged the west country of Ireland had led to massive immigration to the new world where the Irish could begin anew to make a life. Most defendants were instead transported to the Penal Colony of Australia. The day finally arrived when the newcomers were to be welcomed to America.

With papers in hand and clutching his meager belongings, John stepped through the 'golden door' to freedom. This land of opportunity proved to be something less than he had expected. His first look at his new home came as something of a shock. The building that he faced bore a sign 'help wanted' and when he took a closer look to see what type of help was required the words 'No Irish need apply' leaped from the page. 'Land of opportunity? It was the first taste of the rampant prejudice that was common among the populace. John would find that the native born hated the Irish because they were Catholic. Riots earlier in the year had resulted in burning Catholic Churches and killing many Irish immigrants. A few Scotsmen had been killed by the mobs who mistakenly believed them to be Catholic. They were, in fact, Protestant.

He angrily forced it from his mind and began a search for lodging for the night. He decided to sleep on it and make a fresh start in the morning. Then he approached a large house bearing a sign 'rooms to let'. He knocked and was admitted by a rather large woman.

"You've come about the room?" She asked. "It'll be a dollar and a half, US."

She conducted John to the second floor and showed him a small room with a bed and washstand and nothing else. "That'll be a dollar and a half a week, In advance!"

John paid the woman and stowed his meager belongings. Like many who had joined the British Army, John had no job skills other than the trade of soldier. He had to find employment.

"Sure, and where can I find a job?" John asked.

"It'll be mighty hard for an Irish to find a job in this town but the Hall is your best bet." She informed him.

"And where is this Hall?" John asked.

"Two blocks down, ask for the Boss. You can tell if you're in the right place by the large numbers of Irish ruffians hanging about." The woman left John to his own resources.

John found the labor exchange as the woman had said. Large numbers of men stood around the entrance talking. He recognized them as Irishmen, mostly fresh off the coffin ships. He inquired of one of the men, a tall handsome Irish fellow, "I'm here for a job." John said.

"You're late! The lucky ones have already been dispatched. I'm tired of waiting around for a job. I'm off to Saginaw Michigan to see the Irish Dragon." The stranger said.

"And who might that be?" John inquired.

"His real name is Charles O'Malley and he's a Cork County man. Everyone calls him the Irish Dragon, but not to his face. He's called 'the boss' and he controls the waterfront."

"I thought that Michigan was inland." John questioned the man.

"Well, it is in the center of the country, but, is also the major port on the Great Lakes." He replied. "All shipping in and out of the West goes through that Port and the boss runs the docks. Not a single thing moves there but that the boss knows about it. He provides the stevedores that move the goods. He's many other businesses that provide employment for Irish such as yourself."

"Sounds interesting,' John said, 'would you care for some company on your trip? John Reilly by the way." John held out his hand to the man.

"Sure. My name is Patrick Dalton and I hail from Galway Bay."

"What a coincidence! I'm from Ardee just up in the hills from the bay. What are the chances of that!"

"Very good, if you ask me. I've heard that half the population has come to America." Patrick answered.

"Yes, a lot of them are starving what with the potato blight." John agreed. I've seen the tenant farmers evicted, turned out on the roads to fend for themselves. Many have a greenish tint to their mouths that comes from eating grass!"

The Protestant landowners had learned that more money could be earned by using their property for cattle and horses then in farming. The Catholic Irish tenant farmers were simply evicted, turned out on the roads and paths of rural Ireland without any resources. Without food or shelter they slowly starved to death by the thousands or sought passage on a 'coffin ship' for America and the 'golden door' where the streets were said to be paved with gold.

"You've heard about the 'green law' no doubt. That man O'Conner adopted the Shamrock as the party symbol and the Queen passed a law making it the death penalty to be caught wearing one." Patrick said.

"It was very silly. They would have to hang the entire country!" John replied. "What O'Conner and his party did was to ask all the people to wear something green on Patty's day."

The day was that devoted to Saint Patrick, the Patron Saint of Ireland. John and Patrick sought the traditional meal of Irish bacon and cabbage served with boiled potatoes. The visited a small establishment and were surprised to find that corned beef had been substituted for the traditional Irish Bacon. Supply of the Irish bacon did not exist in Boston. The small Jewish community provided 'corned beef' as a substitute. They talked as they eat their meal.

"Let's talk to the Captain and see if he will accept one more passenger." Patrick suggested. They found the Captain at Murphy's tavern and inquired on passage.

The Captain agreed to take John Reilly on the trip.

"We sail on the morning tide. The ship is moored at pier nine, just there." The Captain pointed to his vessel.

It was the following morning as the two new friends stood with elbows on the gunwale talking that Patrick suddenly said: "Back home in Ireland they used to call me Paddy but ever since coming to this country I prefer Patrick."

'Yeah, the local buffoons think that all Irish are Paddy and Bridget's." John agreed. "They're really stupid"

John Reilly and Patrick spent the trip to Saginaw talking and striking up a friendship as Irishmen do. They finally approached shore.

The port was bustling with activity when the two men disembarked and went in search of Charles O'Malley. They reached an impressive building bearing a sign with his name indicating his office was on the first floor. They entered and spoke to a clerk who conducted them into the Irish Dragon's office.

A middle aged Irishman with a ruddy complexion, and the map of Ireland written on his face sat talking to his workers. His voice was deep and very loud though he didn't make it so. It was a natural voice that filled the room.

"And who might you lads be, and what are you about?" The Irishman boomed at the two visitors.

They introduced themselves and asked for work. Charles O'Malley eyed them for some time before replying. Both men were taller than most Irish. John Reilly stood over six feet tall and his companion was perhaps an inch shorter. They were a handsome pair and no doubt the Ladies found them attractive. Large biceps showed that they both were very fit and would make good workmen.

"I've need of some laborers for my lumber yard. Have you a place to lay your head?" The Irishman asked.

They admitted they had no lodgings as yet.

"The widow Molly has a boarding house at this address." He wrote something on the paper. "You can read, I suppose?"

It was a reasonable question since the Americans mostly were illiterate at this time and place. John informed the Boss that he not only read English but Latin, French, German and Spanish. The Parish Priest of Ardee had taught him language as well as the Teachings of the Catholic Church despite the law against teaching Irish children such things. The Crown wished to keep the local populace in its place. Latin was the language of the Mass and the other tongues were to be very useful later.

"I know mathematics as well and some engineering." John added.

"And where might you have acquired such skills." The boss asked.

"My uncle, John Hessian, was a soldier of the king. He was an Artillerist and armorer and used the mathematics in the course of his duties." John replied.

"You're hired, both of you. See the foreman at the lumber yard after you've settled in." The Laird dismissed the men.

The boarding house of the widow Molly was a large structure two street's over from the hall. She greeted the men and told them that she did indeed have lodgings available. Reports of a gold strike to the west had depleted the work pool and several of her boarders had departed that very day to seek their fortune. "The room will be five dollars payable when you are paid." She said.

"Aren't you afraid we might skip out on the bill?" Patrick asked.

"Oh no. The boss will see that it's paid." She said firmly. "Dinner is about ready. Put away your things and come down to the table and I'll introduce you to the others."

The other boarders were a lively bunch, mostly Irish with one Prod, a Scot. The dinner conversation centered with the Texan problem. The newspapers had been reporting that its Annexation was eminent. Newly elected President Polk had received emissaries from Sam Houston to negotiate just that matter. Britain and some other European Powers had recognized Texas as a separate country and the British were meddling in Texas affairs. The situation was reaching a boiling point. Nine years earlier the Texans had defeated Santa Anna and the Mexican Army and set up a new country. Congress was at that very moment voting on Annexation. The question of the slavery issue came up in the conversation and some one of the diners pointed out that a compromise had occurred that would allow the vote to go forward. The Annexation of Texas was a pretty sure thing. Talk continued for over an hour before the boarder's slipped away to their beds.

TWO

The next day they found the foreman at the lumber yard and began their job. The two men worked well together and the foreman was pleased with their job performance.

The work at the lumber mill was a fine job for an Irish laborer and it helped them stay in fit condition. They buzzed the trees into timbers and later delivered them to customers on the docks or at new construction sites in the town which was growing rapidly. I was long hard work and John was soon dissatisfied with the job. He longed for a change.

Congress had ratified the Annexation of Texas and granted them entrance into the Union. Emotions ran high in the country and especially in the North. The Industrial North feared that it would result in yet another 'slave' state to tip the balance of power.

War clouds were gathering on the horizon as the country forced the Mexican Government to issue a stern warning to the Americans that they would not recognize Texas as a separate country or as a State of the United States.

Talks in Washington with the Queen's minister were going the American way. President Polk had issued a challenge to the Crown. He wanted the border with Canada to be draws at fifty four degrees and forty minutes of latitude and the Queen's Emissaries refused this demand. That line was the southernmost boundary of Russian Alaska. The question was settled when the border set agreed on to be set at the forty-ninth parallel. War with Great Britain which neither party wanted was avoided by a mutually agreed compromise.

The long winter was ending and the first green shoots were pushing up in anticipation of spring. John had listened to the war talk around the supper table and a growing longing for the Army life led him to consult with Patrick. He broached the matter quietly to his friend in the privacy of their room. Patrick was agreeable with John's proposal. In the morning they approached the boss.

"Boss, Patrick and I have decided to join the army. We are going to cross the river and ask at the Fort." John informed his boss.

"You've decided?" O'Malley asked.

"Yes" Both men said.

"I've grown fond of you both, but if you must go, then go." O'Malley said.

The friends left Charles O'Malley's office and crossed the river and went to the gate of the post. They informed the sentry that they wished to talk with the Commanding Officer of Company K, United States 5th Infantry regiment.

They were shown into the Captain's Quarters. The Captain, Moses Emory Merrill sat with his feet towards the fire. "How may I help you?" He asked politely.

"We've come to enlist." John explained. He went on to describe his service and rank of Sergeant Major in the British Army.

"What unit did you serve in and where did you serve." The Captain asked.

"Sure, and I was with the 84th foot and we campaigned in India, Afghanistan, and Africa." John answered truthfully.

Patrick presented his resume of duty in the British Army and Captain Merrill was impressed by their record. A stern disciplinarian, he reserved his opinion of the men until he measured their performance men in the field.

"The pay for your grade is seven dollars a month but all your needs are taken care of by the Army. Three hot's and a cot to each soldier. Sergeant Major, get them bunked down." Captain Merrill ordered. John Reilly and Patrick snapped to attention in the British Army method and saluted their new Captain.

"No, that is not the correct way to hand salute. Here, let me show you." He brought John's hand to face his cheek and positioned it at the correct angle for the American style salute. "There, that's how it's done."

The barracks were constructed from rough-sawn lumber and were unfurnished except for a fireplace in which a blazing fire had been started to ward off the evening's chill. The rows of cots were fashioned from rough planking. A meal had been prepared and sat steaming and bubbling in a large pot on the fire. A weathered old soldier ladled out stew onto mess gear. Tomorrow the two friends would begin training but this evening they relaxed and talked with the other soldiers. Introductions had been made and then the talk turned to the Texas Problem.

"The Annexation of Texas guarantees there will be war!" The old soldier spoke softly.

"Surely they will exhaust all means of avoiding conflict." Another soldier spoke his opinion.

"Haven't you read that malarkey that John O'Sullivan is spreading about 'Manifest Destiny'" John asked.

"Mister Polk is determined to possess the entire continent from sea to shining sea. He has made an offer to the Mexican Government to buy the lands all the way to California." The old soldier explained. "They will not sell and it is a grave insult to that prideful people. Only War can wrest those great lands from the Mexicans."

"I heard a rumor that the 5th has been ordered to the border area." Another soldier related.

"So be it! If it's war it takes, then war it will be." John spat. "Think of the promotions that will bring! Perhaps I may achieve my former rank?"

Patrick had listened quietly to this exchange and then he spoke: "Mark my words, if it comes to war it'll be the Prods against the Catholics."

A hush fell over the tent mates as each man considered this pronouncement. Would it come to that? Soon they would know. When the day's drill was completed, Captain Merrill assembled the Company. "Men,' he began, 'we've been ordered to join the Army of the Southwest at New Orleans for shipment to Texas. President Polk has decided on a show of force to the Mexicans. Their Army is, even now, at Matamoros conducting drills on their side of the river Rio Grande. We leave tomorrow on a steamer down the Mississippi river to New Orleans. Prepare yourselves for the trip. This could mean War!"

The day dawned bright, clear and cold. The Michigan winter hadn't completely lost its grip to spring as Company 'K' of the 5th Infantry Regiment embarked on the voyage to New Orleans. The Officers stayed in their warm cabins allowing the enlisted ranks to roam the ship. The vessel was a steam powered paddle wheeler that required stops to replenish its supply of fuel. Men formed a long line and passed the wood aboard to speed up refueling. Some men moved amid the civilians on the dock. They saw little of the hinterlands but quite a lot of the settlements along the river.

Several days later the weather moderated and a warm soft breeze softened their time on deck. When they came to the southern portion of the great river they observed their first taste of slavery.

"You mean that slavers raid the African Coast and capture these unfortunate people and bring them to this country to be sold like common cattle?" An incredulous Patrick asked.

"Tis a sad commentary on the human condition, but yes that is the case." John replied.

"Is there no way out?" Patrick asked.

"Yes, well if one of them escapes and makes his way to the northern states where slavery is illegal then they are free." John replied.

THREE

Many hundreds of miles to the southeast, in the Capitol of the United States, a meeting was taking place in the Office of President of the United States. The meeting was secret with only the Secretaries of State, War and the Treasury present. The subject of the meeting was how to persuade Mexico into giving up her claims to Texas, New Mexico and California. The British were about to offer a compromise on the Oregon Territory after receiving the President's threat of 54-40 or fight. His Northern border about to be ratified by the British Crown of Queen Victoria, James Polk turned his attention to the Southwest.

"So, Mister Secretary, the Crown has agreed to honor out claim to Oregon?" Little Hickory asked.

"Mister President they have agreed to a line drawn from our present border with Canada straight to the coast of Oregon." The Secretary of State replied.

"Then that brings us to Mexico. Have you looked into that story the Mexican Colonel brought up from Santa Anna in Cuba? Is this thing with Santa Anna genuine?" President Polk asked.

'It would appear so, Mister President. For seven million dollars, Santa Anna will return to Mexico and seize the reins of power whereupon he will sue for peace. Then, when he is firmly into office, he will discuss the sale of California to us'" The Secretary of State informed the President.

"Is this Colonel available?" The President asked.

"He is waiting outside the door."

"Ask him to enter." President Polk said.

"Your Excellency..."

"Yes, yes... I know. You're here at Santa Anna's request. I've heard all the details." President Polk said irritably. "Is it true that your General Santa Anna is willing to make the peace for the sum of seven million dollars and, after he is in office, he will sell us California?"

"No Sir!" The greasy little man spat. "The sum was ten million dollars!"

"Ten million?" The president stared blankly at his Secretary of the Treasury who would have to provide the funds. "And when would this action take place?"

"As soon as possible! I have a fast boat waiting to return me to Cuba as soon as I have your answer." The Cuban replied.

"Please return to your quarters. When the arrangements are completed we will contact you there." President Polk took one small step over the line. He would try to bribe the Mexicans out of a war using the public treasury for his funds.

"Get me that Marine Lieutenant, what's his name?" President Polk asked, "Yes, Gillespie, that's it." He pointed to the Secretary of the Treasury.

A tall US Marine, an aide to the president entered. He was assigned to the White House and the President as an Aide.

"Lieutenant Gillespie reporting as ordered." The Marine saluted.

"I have a mission for you, Lieutenant." The President of the United States informed the Marine. "You are to select two men and together you will sail for Cuba with Mister Quick of the State Department. You will protect the large sum of specie that we are sending to Santa Anna. Mister Quick will handle the transfer of funds once you arrive in Cuba."

"Mister President, may I speak freely?" The Marine asked.

The President nodded in answer.

"There's likely to be a war with Mexico and my friends of the First Marines have been ordered south. I would hate to miss it, sir, and since I'll be in the vicinity could I be assigned to the First Marines?" Gillespie held his breath, surprised at his boldness.

"Can't wait to join the fray, eh? Yes, Mister Secretary, cut the orders assigning our war dog to the Marine Expeditionary Force." A rare smile crossed the President's Face. "Take good care of Mister Quick and the money and when you have finished that you can 'see the Elephant.'"

"Thank you, Mister President!" The Marine was dismissed.

The following morning the Marine Officer, his two enlisted men, and the State Department Agent accompanied the Cuban Colonel and ten million dollars in gold to the Port of Baltimore where they boarded the fast packet boat for Cuba. That same day the 5th United States Infantry formed for muster.

"Men," Captain Merrill began, "we're embarked on a voyage to New Orleans where, as part of the Army of Observation, We shall march to a place called 'Kinney's Ranch' where we will be joined by the 7th Inf and other units. Some call the place 'Corpus Christi' which is how the Mexicans know it. Any questions?" No one answered. "See to your troops."

Whispered conversation filled the ship as the troopers packed their kit-bags in preparation for the journey down river. A young Private approached John Riley. "Is it WAR then?" He asked.

"Nay, tis diplomacy. Mister Polk is trying to force the Mexicans to cede half their country. Our Job is to sit and watch and to protect the Texans, not that they need protecting. We are a threat to the Mexicans and the President hopes the Mexicans will think twice before going to war." John told the Private. "Mexico has the upper hand in the matter. They have a first rate army who have been fighting wars for the last 20 years. They number about 40 or 50 thousand while the US Army's strength is just over 8 thousand. So you see we are outnumbered five or six to one.

No, I don't think Mister Polk is really thinking of all-out war."

"You're wrong, ya know." Patrick Dalton a ruddy Irishman and John's friend said. "These Bloody Yanks think they can whip anybody. Didn't they whip the British not once, but twice?"

"Patrick Dalton, do you think Polk will challenge that great army of Mexico?" John asked. "I'm certain Polk means war if the Mexicans don't give him their land. Oh, he's right willing to pay for it to avoid going to war but if the Mexicans refuse......."

"Then why didn't you tell him that?" Pat pointed at the young soldier.

"Didn't want them worrying about the war until the proper time."

Patrick Dalton nodded his understanding. "It'll be a long trip? How long will it take us to get there?" He asked.

"Month or two. It's about 2500 miles twixt here and New Orleans so at the rate this tub moves and depending on the number of stops, I say at least a month." John scratched his chin. "It's about as far as Russia to the Ould Sod."

"This ain't a trip, it's an Argosy!" Patrick exclaimed.

FOUR

Almost one month to the day Company K, 5th Infantry rode the long boats from the Alabama to the Texas Shore. A parade ground had been hacked out of the scrub and the company pitched their tents on its edge. Now would begin the endless drilling of the units to prepare them for war. Something else began about this time. Nativist Officers switched to physical abuse. Any foreign soldier was chosen for punishment for the most minor offense. Punishments included 'Bucking and gagging, the wooden horse, flogging and hanging the offender by his thumbs. The foreign soldiers were singled out for the worst punishment. Nativist West Pointers punished the Irish soldiers more harshly than the other soldiers for real or imaginary offenses. Soldiers sat in front of their tents with their hands and feet bound and a pole thrust between their arms and legs. A gag was forced into their mouths and they were forced to spend the day trussed up like chickens. One veteran soldier automatically corrected his officers drill command to the correct method and was 'bucked and gagged' for his unintended slip.

"John, I don't think those officers know what they are doing. They seem totally uninformed on the subject of battalion and regimental formations." Patrick Dalton observed.

"Aye, but just you have a look at the Artillery!" John said. He was amazed at the proficiency of the flying batteries. The Artillerymen operated in 'battery' as they charged across the parade ground and swung their six pounders around into formation. The Commanding Officer drilled the teams until they reached perfection. Major Sam Ringgold had brought his batteries to a fine edge. He was assisted by Captain Braxton Bragg, an ardent Nativist, Captain James Duncan and several others. "How'd you like to face THAT on the battlefield?" John asked.

"They do look formidable." Patrick answered.

Both men watched as F Company marched past them. One soldier was having difficulty with the commands. Suddenly, an elderly man yanked the offender from the ranks and began twisting his ear. The big Irishman howled in pain and struck the man to the ground. Several officers who were standing nearby jumped and bared their sabers.

"Halt!" The command was given by the man on the ground.

The officers assisted the elderly man to his feet. He was the Commanding General, Ole Rough an' Ready, Zackary Taylor. "I don't think this man understands the orders given him." The General observed. "You there!" The General pointed to Riley. "Do you speak this man's language?"

"Sergeant Riley, Company K, Sir." Riley identified himself. "Yes General, I do, and French and Spanish as well as Latin."

"Ask him his name." General Taylor directed.

John rapidly spoke to the offender explaining the trouble he was in and that he had struck the Commanding General. He asked the man's name and company.

"Says he Sam Timmons of F Company, 5th Infantry and he's mighty sorry for having struck you, sir. He mistook you for a Hostler." Riley stated.

"Well, Riley, escort this man back to his Company Headquarters and inform his Commanding Officer that he is not to be punished! Advise him to learn the language, at least the Close Order Drill and the Range commands also."

Patrick stared open mouthed at the retreating General Officer. Many other Micks and Dutchies who had seen the affair were just as amazed. By suppertime all of the troops would hear of the incident. The ignorant Irish soldier had committed a crime that was punishable by hanging or at the very least, a firing squad and the General was forgiving the Irishman because he hadn't understood the situation.

"Heard the latest about Ole Rough and Ready, John" Patrick asked his Sergeant several days later.

"What's the old gentleman done now?" John Riley asked.

"Seems he was taking the evenin' air in front of his tent and whilst doing so he was polishing his sword. And along come this Shavetail who is new to the Command. He offers a dollar if the General will polish his sword after he's done. The General agrees and the officer leaves his weapon with the General. Next morning when he comes back to retrieve his sword he espies General Taylor".

"Is the General in his quarters?" The young 2nd Lt. asked

"I surely am, and I will take that dollar!" the General said as he offered the blade, freshly shined.

"General's one of a kind. No better man to follow into battle, if it comes to that." John said. "I heard that the Brits are betting the General will get whupped if he takes on the Mexicans. Even the Duke of Wellington called Taylor an 'Injun fighter' said he was lacking experience to command a large force."

"I wouldn't be too sure. He has lots of combat experience and was a genuine Hero in the wars in Florida when they fought the Seminole Indians." John said. "If he loses it'll be because he hasn't enough troops under his command."

"Yah, but I heard that reinforcements are on the way. Mississippi Rifles advance units are coming into camp now." Patrick Dalton observed. "That lawyer, Colonel Jefferson Davis who commands them looks mighty mean!"

"Newspapers tell me that the President has called for 50,000 volunteers from the separate State Militias. That's about what the Mexican Army numbers. Their Army has been in battle somewhere for the last twenty years. I think they will give a good account of themselves!" John paused and scratched his chin, "Will Mexico go to war with the United States?"

"The President seems to be forcing them into a war. Texas is only an excuse to conquer Mexico and take her lands. It is very unfair!" Patrick Dalton had seen the clouds of war gathering on the horizon for a long time. "I've a queasy feeling about battling Mexico."

"Been bothered some myself." John Riley admitted. "Doesn't seem right for Irish Catholics to do battle with Catholic Mexicans for Protestant Americans, does it?"

"The way they treat Irish and all Catholics generally is very unfair!' Patrick Dalton replied. "They hate Catholics because of the religion and even more if you're Irish!"

"Well, we swore an oath to serve and that's that!" Dalton replied.

"They made a promise too! Look at the punishment the Nativist Officers mete out to the troops. Foreigners, Irish, Germans and the others are punished far more than the American born. Why, just yesterday Captain Braxton Bragg of the Flying Batteries had Private Flynn strung up by his thumbs 'cause he failed to Salute properly!" John Riley griped.

"They are not all that way, John." Patrick countered. "Look at Captain Robert E. Lee of the engineers or Lt. Sam Grant, the Quartermaster. Both men are fair and just."

"Yes but Captain Bragg called me a stupid 'croppie' and tried to strike me with the flat of his blade." John retorted. "I had done nothing wrong."

FIVE

Far to the North in Washington a Cabinet Meeting had been convened to discuss what action to take next. President James K. Polk was worried and anxious about the Mexican situation. He meant to have the lands of Mexico no matter what the cost. Messages from General Taylor in northern Texas indicated no progress in the stalemate.

"Let us force their hand. Order General Taylor to advance on the Rio Grande River." President Polk ordered. "Lt. Gillispie and Quick should have contacted this Santa Anna by this time and he should be on his way to Mexico."

"But, Mister President, the border of the Texas Department has always been drawn at the Nueces River." The Secretary of State objected.

"Ah, but our Texan friends declared the border at the Rio Grande and that is what Congress annexed." President Polk countered.

"You realize that this will mean war?" the Secretary of State asked.

"Only if the Mexicans wish it." Polk retorted. "Send the order!"

The order arrived at the Army of Observation's Headquarters at Corpus Christi on a sunny day in March of 1846. The Army would change its name to the Army of the Southwest and would decamp for the north bank of the Rio Grande opposite the Mexican city of Matamoros. General Taylor's force of three thousand men which included 378 mounted Dragoons, Major Sam Ringgold's batteries of flying artillery, the Eighth, Fifth and Seventh Infantry regiments and several batteries of 18 pound heavy artillery guns along with a baggage train of some 300 wagons prepared to move on the Rio Grande.

The Dragons, two batteries of the flying artillery and the Seventh Infantry formed the van of the long column which stretched for miles across the chaparral. The Fifth Infantry was situated in the center of the march. General Taylor, perched on his mount which he affectionately called 'ole whitey' passed Company K several times as 'ole Rough and Ready' surveyed his troops. The column was making good time and marching in good order until, on the third day, it came to a sudden halt.

General Taylor spurred his mount to the head of the column. "Why has the column stopped?" He demanded.

"Mexican Officer with a flag of truce." Captain Thornton of the Dragoons informed him.

Arroyo Colorado separated the Mexican Force and the Americans. Drums, bugles and troops marching and the shouts of their officers and non-coms could be heard coming from the other side of the river.

A tall Mexican Officer dressed in the finest uniform any of the Americans had ever seen trotted halfway into the river. "Sir, any attempt to ford this river will be an act of hostility! You are on Mexican soil uninvited and I must ask you to leave." The Mexican sat patiently waiting an answer.

"Major Ringgold! Deploy your batteries shot with grapeshot. Seventh Infantry, skirmishers out. Prepare to ford the river… and Major Ringgold, if even one shot is fired you will salvo the opposite bank!" Ole Rough and Ready was angry and refused to be intimidated by the Mexican Officer. "Captain inform that Officer he had better get out of our way!"

Captain Bragg took a musket from one of the soldiers and aimed close to the gaudily dressed Mexican Cavalrymen. The Mexican's horse jumped as the shot was fired, but he quickly brought it under control and as he turned, he waved his plumbed hat in salute, and raced for the other shore.

The racket from the opposite bank increased as the Seventh Infantry began to enter the river and soon reached the mid-point. Soon the advance elements were on the other side and loud shouts and laughing could be heard.

"General," a Captain called from the other side of the river, "they are showing us their backs, and they're just a purty as tother side!"

The first confrontation of the Mexican-American war was over without a shot. Matamoros lay just 30 miles away. The date was the 28th of March 1846.

The Army of the Southwest settled in to its encampment on the banks of the Rio Grande. The tiles roofs on the Mexican Town were plainly visible from the camp and the Cross atop the Cathedral shown like a beacon to the Irishmen of Taylor's Army.

Construction was begun on an earthen breastwork and fort. Company K was detailed to the building of Fort Texas. Mexican women came to the river to swim and wash clothes every day. American soldiers began to swim on their side of the river until one brave lad swam clear across the river and disappeared into the town.

Fearing large scale desertion, General Taylor ordered a guard be mounted on the river bank and any soldier passing the center of the river be challenged to return. If that soldier continued to cross the river he would be killed. None attempted to cross for some time. The American Soldiers were content to watch the nude beauties bathe and wash their clothing in the Rio Grande.

Supplies were running low and General Taylor decided on an expedition to his supply depot up river from Matamoros at Port Isabel. He ordered the Quartermaster's department to form a supply train to go for supplies.

General Taylor took a large detachment of troops and went to secure his supply depot a few miles upriver from Matamoros. Point Isabel was isolated from Fort Texas by a narrow dusty trail. It was an ideal point of supply except it was far from the rest of his command. While Taylor was away trouble began.

Sunday was a day of rest for the Yankee Army. Many soldiers went to Church services but the Catholic's had no

Chaplains to offer Mass. Congress had authorized Catholic Chaplains during the Revolutionary War but none had been authorized by the War Department. The Irish Catholics had no spiritual guides in the Nativist Army. An Irish Suttler who owned an outlaying ranch provided a solution.

John Riley and Patrick Dalton decided to visit the ranch house where a visiting Mexican Priest was holding Mass. They left the company area and walked to the ranch. The jolly Irishman welcomed them and introduced his daughter and the Priest.

"This be my daughter, Kate and this is Father Velasquez." The old gentleman explained. "The Father will be conducting Mass for those who wish it."

John glanced around the gathering and was surprised to see many men whom he knew. There was Timothy O'Toole and Sean Connaught from Colonel Harney's 2nd Dragoons. Corporal Callahan from Company B of the 7th and many others were assembled to hear Mass and go to Confession.

John Reilly felt the need for absolution and approached the Priest.

"Hear my confession, Father?" John asked the priest who nodded to John's request.

"Bless me Father for I have sinned." John began.

"And what is your sin, my son?" the Priest asked.

"I took an oath to serve my adopted country, Father, and now I find it hard to keep the faith with that country." John said simply.

"And why is that?" The Priest asked.

"'Tis the treatment the native born officers and noncoms heap on the Irish and other foreigners, heaping verbal abuse, calling the Irish paddy, bog hopper, Papists and such. Then when they punish it seems that the Irish get more than their share." John voiced the complaints of all the men. "The German and French and any foreign born troops are also abused. Many times the abuse is the worst sort of physical torture that one can imagine. So I am tempted to ignore my vow and run away."

"Did they promise you anything when you took the oath?" The Priest asked.

"Yes Father, good food, they give us sour meat and bisquets, good treatment, they mete out unequal justice, good quarters, our tents are worn out. They've kept none of their promises!" John spat.

"Well it seems to me that for an oath to be valid that both sides must keep to their promises." The Mexican said quietly. "Your thoughts are not sinful, my son."

"Father I am a soldier and that's all I am and the worst thing a soldier can do is desert his tent mates. But, lately, I've been thinking what a terrible thing it would be to have to fire on fellow Catholics." John Riley said softly. He was looking for a way out of his predicament and the Priest wasn't helping.

"I cannot tell you what course of action you must take. That is for you and your conscience, and for God. The answer will come in time." The wise old man said.

"Thank you, Father. What is my penance?" John asked.

"None! You have not sinned … yet. Go with God, my son.

John had gone to the Priest with the hope that the old man would suggest a way out of his predicament. He had been disappointed. When John witnessed a soldier punished unfairly because he was a Catholic his Irish came up. He controlled his anger but knew that sooner it would boil over and he would explode.

SIX

"John! John!' Patrick roused him from his thoughts. "The party is starting without you."

Kate and her father were pouring large portions of the potent Irish booze known as 'poteen' and the two boys from the 2nd Dragoons were very intoxicated.

"Come Patrick, we have to be getting back to our billet." John said as he guided his friend towards the camp site.

"But John! I'd like to stay and sample some strong drink." Patrick whined.

"You'll thank me in the morning." John said, not realizing the truth of his words.

The next day began normally enough. Reveille sounded at 4am and the Company began another day of training. It was several hours when John noticed that something was happening at the 2nd Dragoon's bivouac. The entire Company was drawn up in parade formation. Colonel William S. Harney rode up and began addressing the assembled troops.

"These two soddies were apprehended last night when they returned from their midnight revel. Both men were DRUNK!' Colonel Harney bellowed. 'Both of these bog hoppers have been apprehended in this condition before. I WILL NOT TOLERATE HABITUAL DRUNKNESS IN MY COMMAND! Therefore, these men will be punished for their misdeeds as follows. Private Timothy O'Toole you will be branded with the letters H. D. so that all may know what you are. Private Sean Connaught will suffer the same fate but will additionally be branded on the cheek with the letter W to inform the world that he is a worthless soldier. Sergeant! Bring forth the prisoners!"

Private Timothy O'Toole was the first victim of the brand. He was fettered and several of his fellow soldiers were ordered to hold him down. When he was secured the Colonel gave the order. "Sergeant, apply the brand!"

The sickly stench of burning flesh drifted towards John Riley. The screams of the branded soldier echoed in his ears. This was not right! Even the hated British never applied the brand to miscreants! John turned away from the sickly sight. He knew what He must do!

Hostilities had not commenced as yet and John knew that he would have to make his move before the shooting war started. Many foreign soldiers had already deserted and, with the treatment meted out to them, many more would slip across the river to the Mexican side. John knew that he must decide soon!

Waves of excitement, apprehension and disgust swept throughout the garrison. Whispered conversations between the enlisted soldiers increased tensions among the officers and noncoms. Tension was high when an event occurred that took everyone's mind off the matter of the branded offenders.

Clouds of dust and the thunderous beat of horse's hooves signaled the arrival of the Texas Rangers. Each man's costume was different with the exception of boots, hats and weapons. Every Ranger carried two holstered pistols and a rifle such as none of the assembled soldiers had ever seen before. The sat their mounts with the easy familiarity of men who lived in the saddle. The Texas Rangers had battled the Mexican Army and the Indians for 20 years or more and were rumored to be the 'toughest men alive' according to some who knew them.

"Where can I find General Taylor?" The leader asked.

"Yonder, other side of the parade ground. He be the man wearing the duster and the hickory shirt. He has a great shock of white hair but you can't see it for the straw hat he is wearing." John replied.

"Thankee." The big Texan said.

"Sir, who are you and what kind of pistol is that you're carrying?" John asked before the Texan could ride off to see the General.

"Captain Sam Walker, First Texas Ranger Company, and this is the new pistol manufactured by Mister Sam Colt of Patterson, New Jersey. It loads five rounds of .44 caliber ammo and is accurate to a range approaching that of your musket." Captain Samuel Walker informed John. "Come by after we are settled in and I show it to you."

"Thank you!' John stammered.

"Your name?" Sam Walker asked.

"John Riley, Sergeant, Company K, of the Fifth Infantry." John answered.

"Well, John Riley, I will be expectin' you but now I must report to General Taylor." Sam Walker waved his Rangers forward and led the way to the General's tent.

"Look kinda mean, don't they, John." Patrick Dalton observed.

"Heard of them gents before. That Sam Walker helped to design that big pistol he's wearing. Did you notice his rifle?" John questioned.

"Yea, funny lookin' gun." Pat mused.

"It's a five shot revolving rifle. Armed as Walker is, he could defeat over a dozen men. But the armament is only half the story. Those Texas Rangers and some of the toughest fighting men in the world. They've been warring 'gainst the Injuns and Mex's for over twenty years. Hate to face that bunch in Combat!" John watched the Texan talking to the General. "Bet General's got some special mission for the Rangers!"

General Zachery Taylor eyed the Texan who was reporting for duty with his small Army. The General liked what he saw! Sam Walker, Captain, Texas Ranger was tall and ruggedly built with narrow hips and wide shoulders and well-muscled arms. He had been toughened from years in the saddle campaigning against all who would do 'his' Texas wrong. Sam Walker's steady, unblinking gaze told the General all he needed to know about this fighting man.

"When did you say that Colonel Hays would arrive?" General Taylor asked.

"Few more days, about three, I 'spect" Sam replied.

"I have a chore that needs doing now, if you've a mind to." General Taylor said.

"The Rangers are here to fight alongside you, General." Sam said, "Just ask and we'll die trying!"

"My Troops are deserting in droves, mostly the Irish and German Catholics." Rough and Ready informed the Texan. "I would like to have you and your 'mounted Rangers establish roving patrols around the Camp. Some are making a wide circuit around the camp and crossing the river far from our sentry posts. I've given orders for only Americans to be placed on guard and authorized them to shoot to kill any who fail to return after challenged."

"Situation that bad?" Sam wondered. "I've heard rumors but didn't believe them till I seen that Colonel Harney BRAND them two drunks. Anybody tried to do that to my men there would be a lot of blood spilled and most wouldn't be Texan blood!"

It's this Nativist attitude! Most Americans aren't like that but they teach the young Cadets that nonsense at the Point." The General complained. "Any Catholic is fair game but the Irish bear the brunt of the harassment."

"Texans don't judge a man by religion, General. We judge by how good a horseman, how good a roper and how good a shot a man is." Captain Sam Walker told his General. "Why, I even have Catholics serving with me, Mex's too. And every mother's son is a warrior!"

"That is precisely why I want you to ride patrol. If you apprehend any deserters they will get fairer treatment from your Rangers. I'm afraid that the Regulars might shoot the Irish out of hand."

"The Rangers will begin patrolling this very evening." Sam Promised.

John went to see the Texas Ranger and the fancy gun that Captain Walker had promised to show him. It was beautifully made, the product of the finest craftsmanship America could offer. The large 44 caliber ammunition was fitted into specially formed loops in the gun belt. The cylinder spun easily bringing a new round under the hammer with each trigger pull. John handed the pistol back to the Ranger.

"It's a fine weapon! It gives its owner a great advantage over his enemy." John said.

"That it does! I'll match a squad of my Texans so armed up against a full company of the enemy armed with those Brown Bess muskets." The Ranger said.

"Why is it that the regulars aren't armed with those?" John inquired.

"I helped Sam Colt in the design of the weapon and we tried to sell it to the Chief of Ordinance of the U. S. Army but they refused our offer." Sam Walker replied. "They cost about twelve dollars each."

John thanked the Texan and returned to his tent. On the way he observed an Irish soldier being bucked and gagged in front of another tent. John knew he must make his decision soon.

John Reilly requested permission to speak with his Command Officer, Captain Merrill. "Sir, I wanted to request a pass so that I might attend Mass at the farm over there."

"Well, I see no reason why you shouldn't have one. You've been a good soldier and your conduct has been exemplary." Captain Merrill signed the pass and handed it to Reilly.

John saluted and left the camp. He traveled up river until he was well clear of the camp's perimeter and was almost to the river's edge when he was stopped.

Captain Walker of the Texas Rangers asked John what he was doing for far from camp. He handed the Ranger his pass and the Ranger glanced at it and handed it back. "Be back in camp before dark. Wouldn't want one of my men or a sentry to shoot you be accident."

Reilly found a dense copse of vegetation close to the river bank where he would not be observed and concealed himself to wait for the night to close over the encampment.

John Reilly slipped into the Rio Grande River and swam against the current to the Matamoros side. He evaded the sentry's and made his way into the town. He sought the large cathedral in the center square and watched the entrance. After some time he made way to the door and entered. The church was empty of people and only one priest stood lighting candles. He approached the Mexican and asked if the priest would hear his confession.

"Bless me Father for I have sinned." John began.

"You're Irish!' the priest said in alarm. 'I cannot offer sanctuary. The Mexican government has declared war on the church. They raid our churches and carry away the valuables. If they find you here they will simply take you in charge and throw you into prison."

The priest, a pained look on his face looked up as a Mexican Officer accompanied by armed soldiers entered the church. "You're Norte Americano?" The officer asked.

"Si Senor, Sergeant Riley, late of company 'k' of the 5th Infantry. I have deserted my unit and now seek asylum." John answered.

"Take him!" The officer ordered. Two soldiers obeyed the order. He was escorted to the prison and placed in a cell.

John Reilly remained in prison as each day other deserters were captured and brought in to his cell. Many were Irish but there were a few of other nationalities. One man was German and another was British. They languished day after day awaiting an audience with the Commanding General, Francisco Mejia. At long last The Commanding General was removed from command of the troops and replaced by General Pedro de Ampudia who sought immediate changes in the treatment of the deserters. John, who was the ranking American prisoner, was brought before the Mexican General.

"Why have you come to my country?" General Ampudia asked of John.

"I am John Reilly an Irish Catholic and I've no wish to fire on fellow Catholics. War will come to this country and in that case I would be forced to take up arms against your army. I seek asylum from the Americans. If you send me back I will be tried and executed for my beliefs." John explained.

General Ampudia studied the Irishman for a few moments. His quick mind turning the matter over until he made a decision. "If what you say is true, then join us in repelling the invader!"

"What is it that you propose?" John inquired.

"Let us say that you take up arms for Mexico. You will form a company from those in prison and march with the army. Many of you are former soldiers of other nations and will require little training. You would be commissioned Lieutenant and be in command under a Mexican Officer. Any who refuse would be courts-marshaled and shot."

"Allow me to discuss the matter with the men. I am sure that most would welcome the opportunity to serve Mexico." John bowed.

SEVEN

The dank prison in which the prisoners were kept had no windows and only one small candle lit the room. The chamber was damp and dirty and smelled of years of use. John tried to imagine who the previous prisoners were and what crimes they had been guilty of that caused their incarceration. He knew most of the present prisoners from his time in the American Army. Most had deserted due to the harsh treatment by Nativist Officers. He wondered how many would join him in the new unit. He hoped most of the prisoners would accept the offer.

"So that is the proposal, join and be well rewarded with better pay and treatment or face a firing squad.' Reilly explained.' Each man will receive five hundred dollars and 600 hectares of land at the completion of his service. Is anyone opposed to this offer?"

All of the men accepted the offer and John Reilly asked to see the General to inform him of their decision. He was conducted to General Ampudia's office.

"What sort of unit would we serve in, General?" He asked. "I am an expert Artillerist but most of the men are Infantry and have no such skills."

"You men will serve together in a unit we shall call 'The Saint Patrick's Battalion', Colonel Morales will be in overall command but you shall lead the unit." The General explained. "You and your men will be moved to more adequate quarters immediately and provided with uniforms and equipment. Colonel Morales will meet with you after siesta. You are free to move about the town for now but the hostilities will soon begin so keep your men ready to serve."

John was amazed at the opulence of his quarters. A large soft bed was centered in the equally large room. He had never had such lodgings in his life. The walls were decorated with large paintings of excellent artistry. An overly large window allowed a view of the courtyard.

He flopped down on the bed and was surprised at its comfort. He was considering the sudden reversal in fortune when a knock came at the door. "Enter." He barked.

A small Mexican entered, his arms piled high with clothing. "Your uniforms, Senor." He laid out John's new uniforms complete with his rank and then handed John a sword. It would serve both as a badge of rank and a weapon. "Compliments of the General." The man said.

"Mucho Gracias, Thank the General for me." John began to don his new uniform and then he strapped on his new sword. He had worn one before as a Sergeant Major in the 84th foot but it was much plainer than this one. He placed the kepi on his head and left to visit the town.

John was awed by the tall buildings that lined the streets. It was siesta time and few Mexicans were on the streets. He marveled at the various trees and plants that grew in the courtyards of the houses. He recognized none of the subtropical plant life but enjoyed the fragrance that rose from the flowers. He then turned to go to the General's quarters.

John arrived at the general's office and informed the orderly of his presence. The door opened and a tall officer entered the room. He was tall and trim with the body of a professional officer. His appearance was more that of a Spanish Grandee than that of a Mexican. He introduced himself. "Lieutenant Riley? I am Colonel Morales and you will serve under my Command. Among other units I have responsibility for the Field Artillery and that is what I wish to talk about."

"I was an Artillerist with the British Army and rather good at the trade." John replied.

"Perhaps you could train my men?" Colonel Morales asked.

"What is their problem, the mathematics?" John questioned.

"That is the problem. The men are conscripts and most cannot read or write. None of them has even seen a field piece and none of them knows anything about the mathematical equations necessary to sight a gun." The Colonel answered.

"When shall we start Colonel" John asked.

"In the morning. Meanwhile take in the sights. Especially enjoy the parada in the town square." Morales suggested.

"It's a sort of mating ritual. Everyone moves in the opposite direction, boys to the right and girls to the left. The girls walk with the chaperones and look at the boys, searching for a prospective husband. It's quite charming really and part of Mexican life. You will enjoy watching. That I am sure of."

John took the Colonel's advice that evening and selected a view of the square at a café overlooking the Parada. Lines of young people strolled leisurely around the large central square of Matamoros. On several occasions he witnessed a young lady speak to her chaperone about one of the boys. At a later time, if her parents agreed, a marriage broker would approach the suitor with an offer of marriage. It was all very charming and rigid.

While John was enjoying the spectacle taking place below him, Colonel Terrejon and his company of cavalry quietly slipped across the Rio Grande north of the American lines and into the back country. His Command remained close to the river taking up position at a ranch and concealing themselves in the brush that lined the waterway. They would remain in hiding until nightfall when they would began a spoiling campaign against the invaders.

The intelligence the Mexicans had received proved to be accurate. General Zachary Taylor had departed for the major supply point north of Fort Texas which he had placed under the command of Major Brown. General Taylor had been on the road for several days before he received reports of the Mexican forces on his side of the river. The General dispatched Captain Thornton and his Dragoons to intercept the force.

The handsome Captain of Dragoons held up his hand to signal the halt. He surveyed the ranch and its open spaces and decided to rest the troop. His men numbering 68 were ordered to dismount and graze their horses.

Captain Thornton, a graduate of West Point, was a tall handsome Officer who commanded the respect of him men. He was taller than most of his men at six feet and had broad shoulders and trim hips. He looked as a Cavalryman should.

When all the men were afoot and some had loosened the horses girth straps the attack began. The Mexican horsemen charged from cover firing their weapons and brandishing their sabers. The fight was over quickly and ended with the surrender of the Americans who had lost 13 men killed and the other 57 captured. Only one man escaped and he galloped back to Fort Texas as fast as his horse could carry him.

"Major Brown, our entire force has been taken by Mexican Cavalry at the Hacienda on the fjord of the river. We lost a dozen or more men killed and the rest captured." The Trooper reported.

"This must be reported at once! Get that Texas Ranger and have him report to me at here." Major Brown instructed he adjutant.

He instructed the Ranger to ride 'like hell' for General Taylor's force and convey that hostilities had commenced. He had selected the Texan for the assignment because of his ability to infiltrate enemy lines. The horseman slipped through the gate and rode off in a cloud of dust. Shots were fired in his direction but the Mexicans missed the man because he leaned far to the other side of his horse like a Comanche. He rode bravely on towards his destination.

Mexican infantry and some artillery had crossed the river and proceeded towards Taylor's force. The artillery began a cannonade of Fort Texas. The solid shot bounced off the thick earthen walls with little damage. Major Brown stood on the parapet directing return fire which did cause some damage. One shot found its mark on a Mexican gun and wiped out the entire gun crew. John and his company took up the position of the former gunners and began to return fire.

"John, look!" Patrick Dalton shouted and pointed to a gun position where an American Officer was directing fire.

John Reilly took charge of the gun and swiveled it in the direction of the exposed officer. "Fire!" He ordered. The round found its mark and Major Brown fell dead on the spot.

An intense cannonade continued for several hours until approaching darkness and a huge billowing cloud of smoke obscured the targets on both sides of the lines. Exhausted gunners were resting awaiting further orders. Cook fires began to lighten the night sky as only few intermittent shots shattered the night's peace. War had begun between Mexico and the United States.

Hostilities had begun on April 24 when the Mexican Cavalry had crossed the Rio Grande and attacked Thornton's force killing thirteen of this 63 man unit. General Taylor had split his forces and traveled to Port Isabel on the first days of May 1846. On the 8th of May the Texas Ranger arrived with the news of the bombardment of Fort Texas. Taylor assembled his officers.

Zachary Taylor informed his officers of the attacks and first casualties of the war. "Gentlemen, Mexico has spilt American blood on American soil. A State of War now exists." He forwarded news of the attack to President Polk and hastened his long column of troops and supplies onward towards Fort Texas. He dispatched Captain Sam Walker to scout ahead of his force to discover where the Mexican Army was hiding.

"General Taylor, General Ampudia and his Army are arrayed across your route at a place called 'Palo Alto' in a strong defensive position." Sam Walker reported. "I believe I have discovered a flaw in his troop's lines. He has anchored his extreme right flank on a ravine that seems to be impassable but I have found a way around his forces."

"What do you propose Captain Walker?" The General asked.

"Sir, Ampudia has your force outnumbered by three to one. A frontal attack would be very costly. The Rangers could ride far around the ravine and circle into the Mexican rear. If you have your flying batteries lay down a bombardment on the Mexican lines it would cover our advance. At the spot where the ravine peters out we could charge their rear creating panic. From what I see of the enemy force many of the soldiers are untrained conscripts."

"Well, it sounds plausible. Have Major Ringgold report to me and then prepare your men for the mission." Old Rough and Ready instructed.

Palo Alto was a wide plane that gradually rose to small hills. It appeared to be a strong position for defense of the road back to Fort Texas. The left flank of the Mexican line was anchored in a thin grove of trees. A dry creek bed ran parallel to the Mexican front line that would serve as natural breastworks.

General Taylor formed his supply train in the rear of his forces. He placed his Artillery to the van with the Infantry close behind and then he waited for Sam Walker to lead his Rangers to the rear of the Mexican lines. It was several hours before the main body began its march to the battle of Palo Altos. The signal for the charge would be the cannonade that Ringgold's batteries would lay on the Mexican position.

"Mount up." Sam Walker ordered. Any moment the sounds of cannon fire would disturb the peace.

Major Ringgold's batteries charged in front of the Infantry, wheeled and set up their cannon in battery. They began firing canister rounds which caused large gaps to appear in the Mexican lines.

"Charge!" Sam walker shouted as he drew his Patterson Colt revolvers and raced toward the enemy who broke in confusion. "Hit 'em hard boys." He shouted as he drove his horse among the reeling enemy soldiers. They broke and ran in panic towards the dry creek bed. The American Infantry were on their heels and followed the Mexicans into what should have been a very strong defensive position.

Sergeant Major Mick Malone was among the first Americans into the ditch. Two of his company followed him as they searched for defenders. Surprised Mexican defenders bolted for the exit which was a narrow gulch on the left flank that joined a faint trail leading behind the enemy lines. Mick and his men were deep behind enemy lines unsupported by the others from his Company.

Unable to discover any enemy and in a very exposed position, Mick turned and retraced his steps. He would report his discovery to his CO. When the men reached their lines they found that Old Rough and Ready was reforming his Army to continue the advance.

Large clouds of dust kicked up by Zackary Taylor's Army indicated their progress. Enemy Scouts reported their progress to General Ampudia as they approached Resaca de Palma where the Mexican Army awaited the next battle. Mexico's Army which outnumbered the American Army by almost three to one waited. Their gaudy uniforms and quiet demeanor gave no indication of the temerity of the Mexican Infantry who had experienced the frightful accuracy of the flying batteries. Each man waited for the terrible onslaught to begin. The Americans had stopped within sight of the Mexicans. The battle began when the light blue American Infantry marched towards the Mexican line.

Suddenly the Infantry parted to allow the flying batteries of Ringgold, Braxton and James Duncan to race through to the front. The guns wheeled about and went into battery. They were sending canister rounds at the Mexicans. Large gaps appeared in the Mexican line. Soldiers held their formations as they screamed to be allowed to charge the Americans. The Mexican general ordered a cannonade upon the Americans but refused to allow the Infantry to mount the charge.

General Taylor sat 'Old Whitey' calmly in front of his troops as if oblivious to the Mexican arms aimed at him. An enemy shell burst very close to General Taylor who seemed unmoved. That same shell had destroyed one gun of the American flying batteries. Major Sam Ringgold was fatally wounded and fell beside his cannon.

"A little more grapeshot, Captain Bragg." He calmly ordered as if nothing strange had occurred.

Braxton Bragg ordered his Sergeant to take over command of his cannon and gathered several men to right the cannon so recently commanded by his friend and superior officer. In minutes he had the six pounder bulldog back into action.

EIGHT

Far across the battlefield Fernando Gomez who was guarding the Mexican guns pointed to the gun that Braxton Bragg had placed back into service. "See how they fight that gun, Manolo!"

"We would make short work of them if the General would allow our Infantry to advance!" His friend replied.

"No!" Fernando answered vehemently. "They are too quick. By the time our men got to where they are, they would be gone, back behind their Infantry line."

The Mexican defense was in trouble. Their line began to crack and General Ampudia realized he would have to order the troops assaulting Fort Texas to withdraw to Matamoros. He dispatched a rider to deliver the order.

The duel between opposing artillery roared on. Mexican guns fired only round shot which was largely ineffective against the Infantry. The Mexican Artillery was running low on ammunitions.

Just then their Sergeants arrived with the news." We are withdrawing! Everyone is to strike for the river fjord where we crossed. General Ampudia and his staff have already crossed over. Protect those guns!" He ordered. And so the withdrawal soon turned to a general rout. When the Mexican Army reached the river the troopers threw away their arms and jumped into the broad Rio Grande. Many who could not swim were terrified of capture or worse, perished before they could gain the opposite bank. It was a defeated Army that was assembled on the Matamoros side of the river.

The Mexican force besieging Fort Texas had ceased firing and was preparing to withdraw to the other bank of the river. John had prepared several log rafts to ferry his cannon to the other side. Word arrived of the debacle that General Ampudia had suffered at Resaca de Palma and that caused a general panic among those assaulting Fort Texas.

The Mexican Army used civilian contractors to move its heave gear. These men had deserted their post and Reilly forced his men to limber the three guns still serviceable and drive them to the waiting rafts. When loading was complete he ordered his men to shove off and make for the other side. John arrived some distance down river from his position in front of Fort Texas. He parked his battery and went in search of Colonel Morales.

"Colonel, we managed to bring three guns back across the river. Where shall we put them?" John asked.

"Just how did you manage to accomplish that miracle" Colonel Morales asked.

"When we heard of the debacle at Palo Alto I thought it would be better to be prepared in the event the battle went against us." John replied.

"Yes,' the Colonel said. 'That was very good planning. My hopes for victory were dashed when I heard of our Commanding General's refusal to attack. Park your guns in the main square of the town. Be ready to march because the retreating isn't over yet."

"Colonel, may I speak freely?" John asked. The Colonel nodded.

"One reason the American artillery is so effective is that their remount is handled by trained soldiers. Our reliance on civilian muleteers is working against our army. When we began to fjord the river those civilians abandoned their mules and sought refuge in Matamoros. If we had regular troops handling our livestock we would have moved much quicker."

"Who handled the mules if not the contractor?" The Colonel asked in surprise.

"My own men. Some of the men had worked with mules in former service." John answered.

"Hmm, that would be less expensive and provide better management of the animals.

Select men and train them to haul the guns." Colonel Morales ordered.

John selected several dozen soldiers and began training them in the handling of the Mexican mules. They had learned their duties quickly which was important. The following day the Mexican Army began the march to Monterrey while the Americans remained at Fort Texas which they renamed Fort Brown in honor of its fallen commander. It would later be called Brownsville.

The long Mexican Army column marched down the road to the town of Monterrey leaving a trail on dust and injured and dying to mark its passing. Exhaustion, sickness and desertions left the Army depleted of troops. The Saint Pat's kept good order but the Mexican conscripts slipped away from the army and returned to their villages and towns. The Mexican force arrived at the city of Monterrey with little more than half of the men that had started with at Matamoros.

The Army paused to rest at the heights overlooking the valley in front of Monterrey. The city lay off in the distance and seemed a mirage. Strong walls surrounded it and a river wound its way in front of the gates where it meandered beneath a stone bridge less than a hundred yards from the heavy gate. It would be very difficult position for the Yankees to breach.

Colonel Morales approached the cannon on which John Reilly sat resting. "Well John,' he asked, 'what are your thoughts?"

"It seems a very strong defensive position. The weakest point is obviously that stone bridge. If the Yankees fail to take that then the city will hold." John thoughtfully replied. "Their only recourse will be to lay siege to the town."

Colonel Morales smiled. "Those are my thoughts exactly. That is why I am placing your guns in a position to deny the Yankees that prize."

"Sir?" John asked reluctantly, "May I speak freely?"

The Colonel shifted in the saddle and nodded.

"Tis the ammunitions that is in question. We've only solid shot which is fine for knocking down walls but it seems this war will be fought by close-in Infantry actions. The powder is also marginal. It burns erratically causing great inaccuracy of fire." John explained his experiences with his new guns.

"What do you propose?" The Officer asked.

"What I'd like is a fresh supply of powder and some grape and canister shot. Solid shot is not very effective against Infantry, especially at long range. They simply see the rounds and step aside allowing the solid shot to pass through their ranks."

"A convoy of wagons is coming to the city with all you request at this time." The Colonel assured the lieutenant. "I had the same thoughts. I believe that the powder was exposed to the rains and absorbed moisture causing the misfires."

"Give us the tools and we will make the Yankees pay!" John said.

The Mexican Army entered the city in the evening as the sunset bathed its buildings in a soft orange glow. Crowds of civilians welcomed their Army with flowers and cheers. The Bishop and the Alcalde greeted General Ampudia and staff welcoming them to their town. The city had been decorated with banners and bunting and a huge Mexican flag waved about the gate welcoming the Army to Monterrey. A fandango would be given to honor the troops the following day.

The Mexican Army had managed to cover the last thirty-five miles in a single day, a rate of march previously thought impossible. Most Armies only managed ten miles in a single day. It had cost the Mexican's large numbers of troop loss. It would take the American's over a month to cover the same ground.

Colonel Morales and Captain Reilly climbed to the roof of a house that allowed a view of the broad valley in front of Monterrey. To the north lay the road down which the American's would come. West of the city were two large structures that would bar their entry. The first one closest to the entrance to the city was an abandoned tannery and the second one, higher up the valley was the Bishop's Palace. The dark weathered stone of its construction was so dark that the American's would refer to it as the 'Black Fort' since it appeared to be black from a distance.

"There!" Colonel Morales pointed to the Black Fort. "Place one of your batteries at that location. "Who will command that battery?"

"Lieutenant Patrick Dalton, my second in command, would command there, but where shall I site the other battery?" John Reilly asked.

"You and the other battery will be here in the city with my force." Colonel Morales said.

Mexican soldiers were hoisting sandbags to the roof and emplacing them in firing position for the snipers who would be defending the approaches to the city. All of the roofs in the surrounding building were being turned into similar firing positions. Down below them at ground level Mexican's were constructing gun emplacements for three 18 pound guns of John's second battery.

"Colonel, what about that?" John pointed to a spot three miles to the north.

"Bosque de San Domingo?" Colonel Morales questioned. The American's referred to the springs as 'Walnut Grove' although the trees were actually Pecans. Several brooks bubbled from the ground and the tall trees made this a favorite spot for picnics by the locals.

"Yes,' John replied. 'it would be the spot that the American's would choose for a bivouac

Area. Can we deny them the use of it?"

"It's too far from the city. We'll concede that to the Yankees." The Colonel answered.

NINE

Far to the north where General Zachary Taylor rested his troops in the city of Matamoros the US Army Inspected its prize. The City had been conceded by the Mexicans and most of the citizenry had departed with the Mexican Army. American patrols found a large number of prisoners incarcerated in the local prison.

"What are you proposing, Colonel Harney?" Colonel Bliss asked.

"Among the prisoners we have in the prison is one 'Dominguez' who appears to be the ringleader of those criminals. I propose we form a company of spies to infiltrate the enemy's camp and provide intelligence as to his intentions." Colonel Harney explained.

Colonel William Bliss was a West Pointer that had been given the name 'Perfect' Bliss due to the fact that he was an Officer that insisted on striving for perfection in everything he was associated with. He had been number one in his class at the Point and had risen to the top ranks. It was repugnant to him to consider using thieves and murderers in the Army. Colonel Bliss, the Adjutant, reluctantly agreed to put the proposal to the Commanding General Taylor.

"You don't think it would be wise to utilize these men as scouts then?" Taylor asked.

"No sir, I do not! I think it unwise to turn that bunch of cutthroats loose on the countryside. Some of these men were under the death sentence for rape, murder and other heinous crimes." Perfect Bliss replied. "Since they will operate outside of the Army and be under no one's control they will probably go back to their former lives. We will do the Mexicans great harm by releasing them."

"Still we cannot leave them in our rear and there is no one to guard them here when the Army goes to Monterrey.' Zachary Taylor told his Adjutant. 'Much better to employ them as Scouts and spies. Ask Colonel Harney to stop in and see me."

"You wished to see me General?" Colonel Harney reported to the CG.

"Yes Colonel, about those criminals that you wish to employ. I think in is a wise move. I wish you to take charge of that unit. Offer them twenty dollars a month and provide them with mounts, munitions and equipment. We shall utilize them as Civilian Scouts and they will be a part of your Command."

"If they refuse to serve?" Colonel Harney asked.

"Then we shall turn them over to the Civilian Authorities for execution of sentence.

Dominguez had listened to the Colonel and consulted with his fellow prisoners. It was only a moment before they agreed to serve the American Army.

"Just what is your name?" The Colonel asked Dominguez.

"Just Dominguez." The murderer answered. "Only one name."

Colonel Harney closely observed the Mexican Bandito. He was shorter in stature than the average Mexican. His body was hard from the rigorous living on the trail. Dressed in black with silver decorations on his clothing that seemed just about right for his ferocious stance. He wore a Stetson hat rather than a Mexican sombrero and that suited him. All that was missing were the weapons. Colonel Harney was about to lead the Mexicans to the adjutant's tent when the Mexican stopped in the office of the jail.

"Con permiso, Colonel" Dominguez went to the desk and opened a drawer. He tried to open a second drawer and found it locked. He kicked it with the heel of his boot and the flimsy drawer shattered. He reached into the space and drew out a matched set of pistols which proved to be Patterson Colts. He then went to the gun rack and shot off the lock and picked out a strange looking rifle. It was like no other rifle the Colonel had ever seen. It was a custom made sniper's rifle. Dominguez strapped on the buscardero gun belt. "Now I'm ready Colonel."

"We shall have to provide mounts for you and your men." Colonel Harney suggested.

"Chuy, where did they place our caballo's?" Dominguez asked.

"In the stables Jefe." The second in command replied.

The Mexican Scouts found all their horses and equipment and saddles where they had been placed after their arrest. They saddled up and rode to see Colonel Harney.

"The Army will decamp for Monterrey soon and I would like you and your men to scout in front of the column in order to prevent any ambushes on the march. You will operate on your own and will report to me once every day. Draw your supplies from the Quartermaster as needed." The Colonel ordered.

"Si Senor." The head scout answered. He could not believe his luck. The death sentence was gone! And then he was free to wander the countryside and only had to report in once a day.

Colonel Harney, Colonel Hays, Captain Walker of the Texas Rangers and the Mexican bandit met to discuss details of the operations and their responsibilities during the march to Monterrey.

"Captain Walker, you and your men will patrol the route while Dominguez and his lads will patrol a wider area. Skirmishers will cover an area of several miles from the road to insure that no one can surprise the main body." Colonel Harney ordered.

"When shall we begin patrolling?" Sam Walker asked.

"In several days' time. Meanwhile you continue screening the area around the encampment. Dominguez will start his patrols this very day." Colonel Harney answered.

An evil half-smile appeared on Dominguez's face. He and his men would leave on the mission immediately! How stupid these Gringos's were to trust him. He would provide the security but would take advantage of his freedom to scavenge the countryside. The small isolated settlements would pay for the Americans decision to release him.

Dominguez, Chuy and the other bandito spy company rode out to perform a search of the surrounding countryside. The band had traveled some twenty miles without seeing anyone. Then they noticed a plume of smoke far from the highway. The smoke came from cooking fires at a small village where the villagers were preparing the evening meal. The spy company halted to consider their plan of attack. Chuy took half of the men and went to the right of the small town. Dominguez and the rest rode to the left. A single shot rang out before the bandits could get into position.

The locals raced into the largest structure which had been constructed to defend against Indian attacks. The shutters were closed and rifles barrels appeared at the firing slots cut into the wooden shutters.

The Ranger patrol heard the shot and halted to try to discover where it had originated. Captain Sam Walker turned his head and listened for another round to be fired.

Sergeant Wally Carson listened for a moment and then he said; "I think it came from over there." He pointed to the plume of smoke rising lazily over the trees.

The Rangers eased quietly towards the village beyond the bend on the road. Another shot rang out and grazed Wally's large Stetson. Wally returned the fire and could see men hidden in the trees. He aimed his Colt 44 at the one closest to the building and fired. The bandit fell dead.

"Vamoose!" Suddenly the woods were empty. The Rangers searched but found no sign of the intruders.

The Rangers carefully approached the fortress and challenged the occupants to show themselves. An older man opened a shutter and leaned out in answer to Captain Walker's call.

"Hola Senor. They have gone?" He asked.

"Yes, they've gone. Captain Sam Walker of the Texas Rangers and you are…?'

"Senor Jorge Lopez. I'm the headman of this tiny village. Come! My house is yours." The old man welcomed his guests.

"Gracias, but first let me check on this one." Sam pointed to the dead bandito. He approached the man who lay face down on the yard. The bandit was typical of the criminals that roamed Mexico. Government had broken down in the countryside and anarchy reigned.

Jorge came from the house and stood over the dead man. The dead Mexican wore crossed ammunitions belt and a holster that was empty. They soon found the weapon and Jorge picked it up. "Look Senor! Did you ever see such a gun?"

"Yes, it's a Patterson Colt 44 made by Sam Colt and the finest weapon money can buy!" Sam said as he showed one of his two pistols. Sam continued to search the body. "What's this?" He held up the paper the dead man carried to identify himself to American Soldiers.

Just at that moment Wally Carson returned from a search of the surrounding woods. "Sam, you're not gonna like this."

"Yeah, this man is one of that gang of thieves and murderers that Harney released from prison and hired as spies." Sam informed Wally.

"I guessed because everything 'cept the horse and saddle are US Government issue. How did you figure it out?" Wally asked.

Sam held out the warrant issued by Colonel Bliss to identify the dead man. "This spells trouble. These men may be scouting when they are not raiding isolated settlements. This is Jorge Lopez. He's the headman here." Sam waved his hand towards Jorge.

"Look at how he's armed!" Wally said. "Where'd he get the Colt?"

Sam handed the revolver to Jorge. "Strip him of his weapons and if you'll bury him you can keep his horse and anything else you find useful."

"It will be done!" Jorge said. "The pistole, Senor?"

"Keep it. Now I have a question for you. Where are the women and children?" Sam asked.

"Why they are in the mine shaft, Senor." Jorge saw from the puzzled look that the Texan didn't understand. "Come, I show you." He led the Texan into the house and stopped in the main room.

The main room was spacious and furnished with handmade furniture of the highest craftsmanship. A large table filled the center of the room and large cupboards lined the back wall. Jorge went to one of the cupboards and heaved it out of the way to reveal a mine entrance that disappeared into the hillside. Jorge called into the darkness and a light appeared in the distance. A small group of women and children came forward. Jorge rapidly explained to this group that they were safe. The banditos were gone.

"You'll stay the night? It is almost sundown and the roads are not safe at night." Jorge asked.

"Yes. It is rather late to get started today and then those criminals might return to seek revenge on your village. Wally, have a rider return to the camp and advise the Colonel of our situation." Sam ordered. He watched the burial that the local people were doing and was mildly shocked to see that they had stripped the bandit of all his clothing.

"You think that they will come back?' Jorge asked.

"I'm sure of it! We ruined their plans and they will seek to make an example of your village. It may take them awhile since the Army will be moving south soon, but they have to punish you as an example to other villages. They ride in and take what they want and go on to the next town and do the same." Sam explained. "It only works as long as you don't resist them."

The villagers built a large bonfire and the evening meal was taken in the courtyard in front of the large residence. A haunch of beef slowly rotated on the spit. Children played as if nothing had occurred that day to disturb their fun. The roast of beef was delicious and they washed diner down with a very fine wine of local manufacture.

Sam thought that the beef was fine but wondered how simple villagers like these could afford such fare. "Jorge, how is it that you have this beef?" Sam asked.

"When cattle stray into our area we slaughter them and have a feast." Jorge said.

"Back in Texas we hang people for doing that." Sam warned.

"Oh no, Senor. We do not steal cattle. They are wild and roam the countryside and sometimes they come here. They belong to anyone who wishes to take them." Jorge explained.

"Why doesn't someone round them up and start a herd? Seems like you could make a living from the beasts." Sam said.

"It is the Banditos, Senor. Long before you had your herd they would come and raid your property. Many have tried but the bad men make such a thing impossible." Jorge explained.

"Yes, well, we'd better be ready for them should they return." Sam said. "Wally, post outriders so we aren't surprised during the night. Spell them in four hour shifts."

The fire had burned down till only embers remained. "Put that out!" Sam ordered. "We'll sleep outside to be ready for anything that might occur." Sam explained as he unrolled his blankets. "Buenos noches, Senor."

TEN

The first pale rays of the sun appeared over the distant hills as the Texans made ready to ride. Coffee was brewing on the small fire that Wally had started before first light. The men rolled their bedrolls and were saddling their horses when Jorge came from the house.

"Buenos Dias, Senior." He handed Sam a large canvas bag. "For your lunch, Senor."

Sam opened the bag and found plenty of cooked chicken and many biscuits along with a small pot of honey. He tied the bag to his saddle and spurred his horse as he shouted "Mochas Gracias" and rode off. Sergeant Wally Carson guided his mount over close to Sam's.

"You're going to tell the General about that band of cutthroats, Sam?" He asked.

"No. It'd be better to inform Colonel Hays and let him handle it as he thinks best." Sam answered.

The Rangers had the road to themselves. No one was traveling in these troubled days. The rural areas were a lawless territory with small groups of bandits creating havoc. They rode at a leisurely pace and the sun was setting when they entered camp. Wally would see to the horses while Sam reported to Colonel Hays.

"Colonel Hays here is proof that the banditos are the same bunch that Harney let out of the prison." Sam handed the Colonel the paper he had removed from the dead bandit. "They're going to be trouble before this war is over, mark my words."

"We'll just have to keep an eye out for them and that Colonel Harney too." Colonel Hays replied.

"You've heard the stories of his escapades in the Seminole campaign?" Sam asked. "They say that when he captured an Indian camp he would select a squaw to warm his blankets and in the morning when he was through with her he'd have his men hang the unfortunate girl."

"That is not going to occur here. I won't allow it! Keep a sharp eye out and let me know if anything like that occurs. I'll shoot the bastard myself!" Colonel Hays was clearly enraged over the report of atrocities committed by these men. Some of the soldiers who had served under Harney's Command were still serving in this force. Whispered rumors had floated around the camp and Hays had heard them. Imagine a Full Colonel in the United States Army behaving in that manner. Harney would hang an enlisted man for such an offense but he felt entitled to behave that way.

"Mister President, Santa Anna has entered Mexico. As you ordered the embargo allowed his ship to pass through the lines. He has landed in Veracruz and is preparing to march on the Capitol." The Secretary of State reported.

"What of General Taylor?" President Polk asked.

"General Taylor is resting his soldiers in preparation for the march on Monterrey." The Secretary responded.

"We have to keep the pressure on! Order General Taylor to advance on Monterrey!" The President of the United States shouted.

"But sir, General Taylor has done the impossible; He faced an Army of over twenty thousand with a force of only five thousand and defeated them. The public loves the man. There is talk of running him against you on the other ticket." The Secretary of State informed the President.

"Why is it that all my generals want my job?" President Polk asked. "Have General Scott report to me. It is time we opened a second front."

General Winfred Scott reported to the President of the United States. He was taller than most man and was very fit for his age of sixty seven years. He had served his country for forty years and had an excellent record of service. His craggy features reflected long hours on the battlefields and garrisons of the Army. He was the Commanding General of the United States Army and answered only to the President.

"You wished to see me Mister President?" The tall General asked.

"Yes, I wish to discuss your plan to invade Mexico by sea. You believe a landing at Veracruz and a march on the Capitol of Mexico could end the war on our terms?" Polk asked.

"It would have to take place before the miasma sets in. The Mexican's call the summer season the 'vomito' because of the disease that ravages the countryside." General Scott said. "It would have to take place so that we could gain the heights before high summer."

"What is this disease and what causes it?" President Polk asked.

"It is not known what the cause is, but the symptoms are vomiting, fever, dysentery, weakness of limb and general malaise. Half of those who contract it die but the ones who survive seem to be immune to further attacks." General Scott related. "Some call it the 'Yellow Fever' because it turns the skin and eyes that color."

"When would this invasion have to occur in order to avoid this disease?" Polk asked.

"Not later than 1 April. We must have time to reduce Veracruz before we advance inland." General Scott advised.

"Well General, I want you to lead our forces yourself." President Polk gave a wry smile. He knew that Scott had aspirations of getting elected to his office. "Prepare for the invasion of Mexico and take what forces from General Taylor's Command as you feel are necessary."

"Sir, we shall need the cooperation of the Navy." Scott reminded the President.

"Yes you will!" President Polk answered. "That's the reason I am appointing you the Supreme Commander of the invasion including the Army, Navy and Marines. The Navy will march to the tune of your drums General."

"It may be necessary to hire civilian craft to support the landing. Can you instruct the Quartermasters to contract for the required ships?" General Scott asked.

"It will be done. General, have you received any communications from Taylor of his situation?" The President asked.

"None since the message that he was decamping Matamoros for the city of Monterrey." Scott answered. "He should be entering the city about now."

General Scott had made his plans for the invasion almost a year ago. Now it only remained to put them into action. He called a meeting for his staff that afternoon. The Army had blossomed from a force of eight thousand before the war and manning now stood at almost sixty thousand with that number again with the volunteer Militia. It required all of Scott's organizational abilities to bring order out of the chaos. Colonel Bryers, Scott's Chief of Staff for operations arrived first.

"So General Scott, The President has agreed to pursue your plan to invade Veracruz?" The Colonel asked.

"Yes, and I shall be in overall command including the Naval support. Cut orders for all Commands to prepare for shipment and coordinate with the Navy and the Quartermaster Corps to arrange transport for the troop units and marshal the necessary equipment. We are going to war!"

"What units of Taylor's command will you wish to take to Veracruz?" The Colonel asked.

"The Fifth and Seventh Infantry, Braggs artillery battalions and Colonel Hay's Texas Rangers. That'll do for a start. We'll select additional troop units when we arrive at Carmago. I shall also want Colonel Bliss for my Adjutant and Major Lee of the Engineers. See to it!" Scott ordered.

The various troops began loading aboard troopships and the most difficult were the eighteen pounder Cannon and the horses. They were loaded onto shallow draft vessels to avoid having to unload at New Orleans and then reloading onto the shallow draft boats. Troops would remain aboard the vessels and only the deeper hulls would disembark.

ELEVEN

As the Army began its voyage to
New Orleans General Taylor's force began its march to Monterrey. His column consisted of 3200 regulars, 3000 volunteers, along with the artillery and a supply train of over 300 wagons. The army was spread out for miles with the General and the Texas Rangers in the lead. Dominguez and his men rode on the flanks with half on each flank. The Infantry followed closely behind with the Artillery and supply wagons struggling to keep up. It would be a long boring ride.

On September 14th General Taylor rode to a point three miles from Monterrey. The city shone brightly in the strong Mexican sunlight. An enemy 18 pounder fired a solid shot in the General's direction. He sat for a moment before wheeling his mount and returning to his Command at the perfect picnic spot where the troops were establishing a bivouac. It was called Bosque de Santo Domingo by the locals but the Americans named it Walnut springs in the belief that the tall trees were walnuts but they were actually pecan trees. It was a very pleasant bivouac with bubbling springs and small brooks to provide fresh water.

General Taylor called a council of war. The Commanding Officers of each unit joined him under the largest tree. The sound of a babbling brook a few feet away did nothing to soothe the tension that filled the meeting.

"Gentlemen, we have our work cut out for us. The way I see it we will have to accomplish three things before we can even think of attacking the city. First we have to reduce the Tannery and the Black Fort and then we have to find a way for Worth's Infantry and two batteries of Bragg's

Artillery to circle the city and establish a roadblock on the Saltillo road to prevent reinforcements reaching the city. Then and only then the remaining troops will assault the city."

It was obvious that the strategy would work if all units obeyed their orders.

"Major Lee, can you reconnoiter a way around the city that won't get my men killed?" General Worth asked.

"Yes General, I think we can be find a way around that will ensure their safety. I take my Sergeant and leave immediately." Major Robert E. Lee saluted and left on his mission.

Colonel Hays wore a puzzled look. He had questions about the entire operation. "General Taylor, let us assume that we safely capture the Saltillo road and the Forts. Taking that city will be mighty hard to do."

Old 'Rough and Ready was deep in thought. He had seen the fortified sniper positions on the roofs of the homes. The narrow streets would be a bottleneck for the attacking troops. "I'm open to suggestions." The General said.

"Colonel Hays, these Mex's houses are built out of mud bricks that shatter easily, don't they?" Sam Walker asked. "Why don't we have the lead troops carry picks and when they have taken the first building they can chop a hole in the wall so they can enter the next building. When they've taken the first house they will be able to clear the riflemen from the other houses."

General Taylor spread a map onto a table and examined it. The positions of troops were accurate as far as the American troops went, but, the Mexican positions were unclear. A wide avenue led from the entrance straight towards the main square that was rimmed by tall buildings. A Cathedral was centered on the square and other less impressive building rimmed the large open area. The other streets leading in the other direction were narrow and would be a bottleneck for the advancing troops.

"Captain Walker's idea of breaking down the walls is excellent but it doesn't solve the problem with the side streets. Nor does it solve the problem of the enemy's 18 pounders that are in enfilade to the main avenue. Troops advancing down that wide street could suffer a withering fire as they advance." General Taylor was clearly worried.

Major Robert E. Lee returned from his reconnaissance at the same time that Dominguez the scout had arrived. Ever the Southern gentleman, Lee bowed and swept his hat towards the group of Officers. The arrogant Mexican curtly brushed past the Major and began his report.

"The Mexican positions are very strong general. They have a battery of 18 pounders at the square that sweep the entrance to the city. The Black Fort is manned by the Irish renegades with many cannon up to and including those big 18 pound siege guns. The Tannery is also heavily fortified. The same officer who ran at Resaca de Palma commands there and he'll probably run again. Not so the Irish."

"Who is the Commander at the Black Fort?" General Taylor inquired.

"Colonel Morales commands and he is not a political officer but rather a seasoned regular officer who has been fighting Mexico's wars for over twenty years. His second in command is one John Reilly, a deserter from your army. He has a large number of others, mostly Irish, under his command."

General Taylor turned his eyes to Major Robert E. Lee of the Engineers who had scouted a route around Monterrey.

"What did you find Major?" Taylor asked his Engineer.

Major Lee traced a route around the city. "This approach should afford adequate cover around the city with the exception of this area." He pointed to a slight rise in elevation. "As you can see there is about a hundred yards in front of the Black Fort where the troops would be exposed to cannon fire from the Fort. If we move early enough before the light is good, I think we can quick march past before the enemy is aware of our intentions. The range from the Fort would be a thousand yards give or take a few yards."

A satisfied smile appeared on General Taylor's face. "That's it then. General Wool have your column on the move early enough to pass the chokepoint in front of the Black Fort. Colonel Hays I would like Captain Walker and his company of Rangers to lead the assault on the city proper. One company of Engineers will accompany them."

The council of war was over. Now it remained for the army to pass through the night. Some soldiers such as Sergeant Major Mick Malone slept soundly but many others found sleep impossible. It especially affected the untried young soldiers who had joined the force after the battles before Matamoros. An uneasy anticipation kept many from the rest they would need on the morrow.

TWELVE

Most of the Rangers slept soundly, undisturbed at the prospect of battle. They were all veteran frontiersmen having fought Texas' battles with Mexicans, Indians and other troublemakers on the frontiers of Texas. After the long night ended Sergeant Wally Carson shook his men awake. The Rangers saddled their horses and prepared for action.

General Wool's column had been on the move for hours before first light of day and almost skirted the Black Fort when the boom of the cannon sounded. The shot bounced harmlessly across the ground and it was quickly followed by several other shots. The tail end of the column galloped at quick march over the exposed ground without casualties and shortly after gained the Saltillo Road junction. This was accomplished without a single loss and now the city was surrounded and with no way in or out, the other assaults could proceed without fear of interruption.

The Seventh Infantry moved to positions in front of the Tannery and the heavy 18 pound guns began softening up the target. Round after round shattered the walls of the building which was not erected as a fortress. Mexican casualties were many. The American guns were very accurate and had demolished parts of the walls.

The Mexican guns had not been silenced and soon began a bombardment of Mick Malone and the Seventh.

"Charge!" Mick Malone ordered. Waves of powder blue clad regulars raced to the front parting only for the guns of Duncan's Flying Battery to swiftly wheel their guns to within musket shot of the Tannery. The small six pounders began firing at a rate of five rounds per gun, a rate of fire once considered impossible to maintain. The guns were shot with canister that contained many small projectiles that cut through the enemy ranks. The Mexican guns were chopping holes in Mick's company as they sought cover at the outside walls of the structure. Mick was the first man there. He drew out a bomb and lit the fuse and then threw it into the window that had held an enemy sniper moments before. A loud explosion followed by billows of smoke issuing from the window caused confusion in the enemy ranks.

"Follow me lads!" Mick shouted as he leaped into the room. One Mexican who had taken the brunt of the blast lay in the corner oozing his life's blood. Another Mexican was raising his rifle to shoot Mick who shot him first. Two others threw up their hands in a gesture of surrender.

"Look Sergeant!" Mick looked out the window to see a pudgy Mexican Officer waddling away in the direction of the city. All that remained was the mopping up of the other soldiers who had stayed at their posts. Eighteen Mexicans had surrendered and the rest followed their Commanding Officer back to the safety of Monterrey. Mick rounded up his prisoners and sent them to the rear under guard. He gave his man instructions to report to General Taylor that the Tannery had been taken.

General Taylor received the news of the Tannery's capture calmly. "Tell Mick and the others it's a job well done. Leave a holding force in the Tannery and bring the men down to join the assault forces in front of Monterrey."

Mick Malone took stock of his remaining troops. The Company Commander had been severely wounded in the assault and was being carried back to the hospital. This left Mick as the ranking survivor in his company and he quickly assumed full command. His route back to the Base of Operations was safe enough. The guns of the Black Fort were not situated to bring fire on his column.

"General Twiggs, I've been ordered to join your command by General Taylor, what are your orders, sir?" Mick reported to the Commanding General of the assault force tasked with taking the town.

"Where is your Commanding Officer?" The General asked.

"I'm the ranking soldier to survive the attack. The Captain and Lieutenant were wounded and killed." Mick explained.

"That being the case Sergeant you are hereby brevetted to the rank of Lieutenant. You will assume command and report to Captain Walker of the Rangers. They are having some difficulty in entering the city. Dismissed!" Mick saluted and went in search of his new command. It came as quite a shock to Mick that he, an Irish immigrant, could achieve officer rank. Some Irish were given command but only the native born and few of those. Only Bennet Riley was given that distinction and he had earned it on the battlefield.

"Lieutenant is it?" Sam Walker asked. "We can use you here. We can't seem to close on the walls of that first building."

"With your permission, Captain. I'll take two men and approach from the extreme right flank and take position at the base of the first house. If you and your men will lay down a covering fire on those roof top riflemen we should be able to make it. Then we'll use one of these." Mick showed Sam a grenade. Once you hear the explosion have your men charge the house."

Sam settled down behind the cover afforded by the ditch like depression in which he and his men awaited Mick's approach. The Mexican riflemen were concentrating all their attention to their front and ignoring the flanks. Mick and his two men crawled out from cover and made the short distance to the wall. Just as they stood up thinking they were safe from the rooftop snipers one of the Mexicans leaned over his sandbagged rifle pit and pointed his rifle at the ground. He had intended to kill Mick and his two men but sharp-eyed Sam Walker noticed the movement. He sighted his Colt on the Mexican and pulled the trigger. The rifle clattered to the earth as a sharp explosion echoed across the field.

The bomb had disoriented the two Mexicans on the ground floor long enough for the two men to hoist Mick and threw him into the ground floor room. One man lay dying and the second Mexican was already dead. Sounds from the roof indicated that the riflemen there knew they were under attack. Sam and his men rushed through the opening and soon they were in position to attack the roof. Mick drew out the grenade and lit the fuse.

"Let me do it." Sam asked. Mick handed the bomb to the Texas Ranger.

The doorway to the roof had been left open for ventilation and Sam pitched the bomb out the open door. The explosion was deafening as Sam hurled himself through the doorway. Dazed Mexicans still reeling from the blast threw up their hands in surrender. The hard part was over. Mexican soldiers on the next roofs quickly faded away.

Mick Malone studied the street below and was amazed at how much easier the going was now that they had neutralized the rooftops. He followed the infantry's progress as they made for the end of the block of houses. Then he saw a civilian closely following the soldiers. The shadowy figure ducked into doorways to avoid the incoming fire. Suddenly Mick knew who that figure was. It was that dammed Dominguez, the Scout. Mick pointed him out to Captain Walker.

"Think he's going to give away our position Captain?" Mick asked.

"Not likely. If the Mexicans catch him they'll swing him from the closest tree! No, he's probably reconnoitering for the General." Sam said. "Let him go. I'd like to shoot him myself but that might interfere with his mission."

"How many prisoners have we collected thus far?" Mick asked.

"A little more than a hundred. Say, why don't you take two squads and escort them back to the rear. Then report to the General our situation." Sam said. "Me and the boys will secure this area and wait for morning. Can't have those Mex's filtering back in to occupy these roofs."

"But Captain Walker, I'm only a second lieutenant." Mick said. "And haven't been such for an entire day."

"It was long overdue. You are a fine soldier and richly deserving of that promotion." Sam said.

"But I'm Irish born and everyone knows that the immigrant Irish cannot obtain officer rank." Mick explained.

"But you've proved them wrong, haven't you." Sam said." Why did you come to this country?"

"Why for freedom, of course. That and a chance to make my fortune, build a house and maybe even have a piece of land to call my own."

"What stopped you?" Sam asked.

"The Native Americans hate the Irish and would sooner hire a freed black than an Irishman. It's because we are Catholic." Mick said.

"Well, when you're through with the army come on down to Texas. We have land a plenty and opportunities galore. Ask at any Ranger Station for me and I'll help you get set up." Sam meant what he offered.

"You are sure?" Mick asked.

"Absolutely! But it will be dark soon and we need to get those prisoners back to the rear. We'll talk later."

THIRTEEN

Mick turned over his prisoners at the PW compound and reported to General Taylor's HQ. Colonel Harney asked. "Who are you and what do you wish of General Taylor?"

"Lieutenant Mick Malone and General Twiggs wished me to report on the situation at the front."

"And just when did you become a Lieutenant." Harney sneered.

"General Twiggs Breveted me a short while ago after we took the tannery and our officers were killed in the attack." Mick replied.

"General Taylor, this bog hopper wishes to report on General Twigg's condition." Harney said. "Lieutenant, bah!"

"And just what is the situation there, Lieutenant?" Old Rough and Ready asked.

"We've cleared the roofs of riflemen on the first block of houses and captured over a hundred prisoners. Captain Walker and the Rangers are establishing a defensive perimeter around our gains."

"General, this man cannot be a lieutenant!" Colonel Harney said.

"And why is that Colonel?" Taylor asked.

"Sir, He is Irish born and a Catholic to boot. There has never been an Irishman in the Officer Corps." Colonel Harney was livid.

"Did you take the oath?" The General asked Mick.

"No sir, there wasn't time with all the fighting." Mick replied.

"Raise your right hand."

Mick raised his right hand and General Taylor swore him in. "There! Adjutant note in the daily report that

Sergeant Major Malone is bereted to the rank of second lieutenant."

Colonel Harney spun around and left the HQ without even saluting the General. The rage he felt showing plainly on his reddened face.

General Taylor sadly watched the irate Colonel Harney leave. "He may be a colossal ass but he is a fine soldier. I couldn't do without him." General Taylor explained.

Dominguez, the spy company captain arrived just as Colonel Harney was leaving. The Colonel hurled an insult at the spy. A sly smile lit Dominguez's face as he considered what he would do to the Colonel if he had him alone.

"What have you discovered in your foray, Captain?" Taylor asked the spy chief.

"The Cathedral is being used as a powder magazine. It is crammed full of munitions and one stray shot from your artillery could set it off. I suggest you inform your gunners to steer clear of it else you will capture a great hole in the ground." Dominguez informed the General.

"Colonel Bliss, get word to all units about that church." Taylor hoped that none of the Nativist such as Bragg might think it fine sport to destroy the Mexican Cathedral.

Lieutenant Mick Malone returned to his unit unsure how his former tent mates would take the news of his promotion. The division between the Officer and enlisted class was absolute. Most of the men already knew of his promotion to Lieutenant and their attitude was one of respect that came not from the rank but respect for the man. Mick could see it in their faces and their salutes. He had earned their respect as an enlisted man and his promotion had enhanced that feeling. Colonel Harney was furious but dared not act against Mick, not after General Taylor had administered the oath himself.

Sleep came easier to the exhausted troops. They had been blooded and each man knew how he would act in the face of enemy fire. With a feeling of relief they lay down to sleep. Most slept easily with no terror from the previous night. Morning came early. The Army was up before first light and joined those who had remained in the city.

Mick found Sam enjoying his morning coffee at the first house. "Morning Sam."

"Here they come. Squads of Mexicans were advancing down the broad avenue in an attempt to retake the area they had abandoned to the Americans. Bragg's artillery fired canister shot at them and they faded back into the doorways.

Door to door fighting began and the American infantry took a lot of casualties until firing ceased about noon. A Mexican Officer advanced up the broad avenue bearing a white flag of truce.

"What do you suppose that's all about?" Sam Walker asked.

"The Mexicans are going to offer terms for surrender to General Taylor." Mick Malone replied. "They have us outnumbered five or six to one."

"The General won't go for that! He'd rather fight to the last man before he surrendered his command." Sam said.

Colonel Bliss rode out of camp and met with the Mexican officer. The two officers conferred for some time and then they parted ways. Colonel Bliss rode back to Taylor's HQ. He explained the terms that the Mexican had relayed for General Taylor.

General Zachary Taylor began to laugh when he heard the Mexican's terms. A three months truce and the Mexican Army would abandon Monterrey to the Americans taking most of their arms and equipment. "Won't that fry Mister Polk's bacon?" He laughed again.

"General, you mean to accept of it?" Colonel Bliss asked. "President Polk will have an apoplexy fit when he hears of it."

"Well Colonel, it's a good deal. The Mexicans will march out of Monterrey with only one battery of guns, the old worn out ones. They will have their colors but little else. We will inherit his stores including the magazine and the majority of his guns. Since they produce no armaments in this country and buy their cannon from England which will be impossible with blockade, we have effectively disarmed the rascal. Let Mister Polk chew on that!"

"Shall I convey your acceptance of the terms to the Mexicans sir?" Bliss asked.

"Yes and get the word to the troops and especially to General Worth at the Saltillo road." General Taylor said. "I shall review the troops as they pass. They can leave after breakfast.

Colonel Bliss rode to the town carrying a flag of truce. The Mexicans listened to the terms and agreed that the retreat would happen at nine in the morning.

FOURTEEN

Night settled over the battlefield as the truce took effect. Bonfires were ignited and the soldiery spent the hours before retreat sounded discussing the battles of the day. The American Army had done the impossible. They had defeated a force many times their size and conquered Monterrey.

Somewhere in the darkness an Irish tenor began to sing: 'Green grows the lilacs that bloom in the spring.' It was a popular song that everyone in the Army knew. The Mexicans were unfamiliar with the song and questioned what the Yankees were singing about. Soon a Mexican voice began a different tune. The Americans didn't understand the words but most liked the tune.

The tune was an Irish song that was popular in the American Army. Even Nativist officers liked it. It rang out in soft notes as others joined it:

'Green grow the lilacs, all sparking with dew
I'm lonely, my darling, since parting with you;
By our next meeting I'll hope to prove true
And change the green lilacs to the Red, White and Blue

The bugle call rose over the American camp and the singing abruptly ceased. Then the soulful notes of Taps sounded through the American camp and a peaceful calm night began. American patrols circled the camp to prevent further desertions by the foreign born soldiers, especially the Irish Catholics.

This precaution would prove unnecessary. Flush with the victory in the lopsided battle, none of the soldiers attempted to go 'over the hill.'

"Captain, why do they desert?" Wally asked Sam Walker on the following day.

"Look!" Sam pointed to a soldier who sat bound and gagged. His hands and feet were tied and a pole was separating the two. A dirty rag was forced into the man's mouth. "Those Nativist Officers hate the Catholic soldiers so much that they punish for little or no reason."

"Yeah, I see your point Captain. Were some officer to do that to me I would have no choice but to kill the bastard!" Wally replied. "Don't them stupid bastards know that you can catch a lot more flies with honey than you can catch with horseshit?"

"Hell, Wally, I'm not sure that's true. Have you noticed the manure piles lately?" Sam Walker laughed. "But it's a good theory."

"Captain, suppose we ride down and watch the grand Mexican Army retreat?" Wally suggested.

The two Rangers rode to the main square where the Mexican Army was drawn up to leave Monterrey. The Mexican colors were flapping in the breeze and the soldiers carried all their arms. It was an undefeated force, one which the Americans would face again later. The Mexican band played martial airs as the Mexicans led by their General and his staff led them from the city.

The gaudily uniformed General and his Staff rode at the head of the column were followed by the Mexican Calvary. Next came the Infantry units which were followed by the Artillery units which General Taylor had allowed the Mexican Commander to keep. Next in line were the infantry. Almost at the rear of the long column were the Artillerist with the Irish deserters riding on the caissons attached to the 18 pounders. Captain Reilly rode on the first cannon.

Loud shouts and boos began in the American ranks as the deserter drew abreast of the American Infantry. Derogatory shouts were hurled at the Irish deserter. Every soldier present knew that far worse than deserting, Reilly and his band had fired their cannons at the American Infantry causing death and injury to his former tent mates. Quite a few of the Infantrymen would have gladly fired at the Irishman but true to General Taylor's command they were allowed to pass unmolested. Many vowed to make the Irishman pay for his treachery! It took several hours for the Mexican force to pass out of the city.

General Taylor and the Quartermaster, Lieutenant U. S. Grant rode to the Cathedral to inspect the stores in the temporary arsenal. Enough munitions for several great battles were stored there. "Lieutenant, Have all this,' Taylor waved his hand over the piles of supplies 'loaded onto wagons and prepared to move with the Army."

Taylor and Grant next went to the Artillery Park where they inspected the captured guns. Many were brand new cannon of late manufacture by English cannon makers. Five of the guns were of little use and all of the cannon were spiked. Gunners drove metal spikes into the priming hole of the cannon which rendered the guns useless in the field, but, an armorer could restore them at his leisure.

"Have Major Lee get an ordinance man over here to clean up these guns. I want them fully serviceable before we leave this city." General Taylor ordered.

Major Robert E. Lee and his expert cannon repairman arrived at the artillery park and inspected the captured guns. "What do you think?" Lee asked.

"It's a simple job, Major. We clean out the fuse holes and resize them for our fuses and they will be ready for action." The craftsman replied.

"See to it.' Major Lee ordered. 'These guns must be ready to roll when the army leaves for the next battle."

"They'll be ready by the end of the month." The Armorer said.

FIFTEEN

While the Mexican Army marched down the road to Saltillo a dispatch rider was sent to Washington and President Polk. It took the rider three weeks to reach the President. He was enraged when he received the news.

"Taylor did what!" James Polk shouted. The news of the in creditable victory had already been reported in the press but no mention of the armistice had leaked out. "Order General Taylor to catch the Mexican Army and destroy it at once. By this time that phony Santa Anna will be using my ten-million dollars to raise an army and try to destroy our army."

The dispatch arrived at Monterrey as Taylor was making plans to decamp for Saltillo and he dutifully dispatched a rider to inform the Mexicans that the truce was to be canceled and hostilities would commence with the receipt of his message. The rider arrived at Saltillo only to discover that the Mexicans had departed for the town of San Louis Potosi. Santa Anna would relieve General Ampudia of his command of the Mexican Army and assume leadership in his own right.

In the American camp all was not well. The Regular troops and worse, the volunteers were creating havoc upon the countryside. Hardly a day passed without a civilian residence being burglarized and its inhabitants raped and murdered. General Taylor sent for the only troops under his command in which he had absolute confidence.

Colonel Hays and Captain Sam Walker reported to the General's HQ. Both men guessed what the General wished to discuss.

"The troops are creating havoc out in the country. Most of the atrocities are being committed by the volunteers but some are being done by the regulars. It seems I am hardly able to control their actions. What we need to do is capture some of them in the act of committing their crimes. I would like you Rangers to establish patrols stealthy to catch some of the culprit's red handed."

"General,' Colonel Hays said, 'Captain Walker here is the man you need. He has lots of experience capturing felons in the act. I would suggest he be given carte blanche in his patrols."

"I'll hand pick some of my men and we'll begin this very evening with your permission."

"Captain Walker, it must be understood that I require live culprits, preferably regulars. They will be courts-marshaled and punished according to the Articles of War. Is that understood?" General Taylor asked the Ranger.

"Yes General, I understand that you'd like to make an example for the others in your command." Sam Walker replied. "We'll take them alive."

Sam assembled the Rangers and selected a dozen including himself. Sergeant Wally Carson would be second in command but all of the Rangers were experienced in the type of action Sam asked them to volunteer to do.

Wally seemed bothered by something and Sam noticed it on his face. "What's up, Wally?" Sam asked.

"Well I was wondering about Hernandez. What's he going to do when he has to fire on other Mexicans?" Wally asked.

"He might look like a Mex and have a Mexican name but at heart he's pure Texan! Did you know that at San Jacinto back in '36 he and his men captured Santa Anna and delivered the bastard to Sam Houston? I'd bet my life on Hernandez!" Sam Walker stated.

"I didn't know that! He fought in the Liberation? Is it true that Santa Anna was dressed in woman's clothes when they took him?"

"I don't know, Wally, Best to ask Hernandez." Sam suggested.

The Rangers studied the map for possible sites that had not already been raided. General Taylor had provided the locals of previous incidents. "Wally, where do you think they are likely to strike next."

Wally pointed to a spot on the map that showed several buildings. "There, it's far enough to not alert the pickets and off the road so as to avoid traffic. That's where I strike if it were me."

"They are not that brave! There must be a dozen or more houses in that small village. No, they are more likely to strike a single dwelling. Sam explained.

"I don't mean the village but see this mark here?" Wally pointed to a building far from the village. "A single family lives there and that's where they'll strike."

The Ranger Patrol left the city just as the sun was setting casting a bright orange glow that bathed the countryside in warm rich light.

Wally edged his mount next to Hernandez. "Is it true that you captured Santa Anna and he was wearing woman's clothing?" He blurted out.

"Yeah." Pedro Hernandez laughed. "It was quite a sight. He'd hidden in one of the wagons and when we found him he came peacefully enough."

"Pedro, I've known you for what, six years, and you never told me about that."

"Nothing to tell." Pedro replied. "We scooped him up and delivered him to General Sam Houston who made him cede Texas to us with the boarder at the Rio Grande. The Mexican Government refused to accept it and they threw that slimy politico out of the country. Sent him and his staff to Cuba to live in exile."

"Dam shame you didn't shoot him when you had the chance! This war might not have been necessary." Wally said.

"Oh, it would have been. The Mexicans would have found another asshole to take Santa Anna's place. That's what wrong with their army. The soldiers are brave and willing to suffer much for their country but then the officers make a mess of it. A hell of a lot of them are appointed politically and know nothing of soldiering." Pedro explained.

The Rangers rode in silence now. They were closing in on the remote farmhouse. A scream echoed through the trees and the Rangers halted.

"Wally, over there!" Sam ordered. He would take the straight path into the yard. A young girl had broken loose from her drunken captor. Blood ran down her cheek from a wound over her eye. Sam used his horse to force the drunken soldier away from the girl. He leaped from his horse and used a piggin' string to bind the soldier's arms behind him and then knocked his legs from under him. "Don't move! How many others are there?"

"Two." The soldier spat.

Sam rushed through the door and found two more soldiers rifling through the owners possessions. An old man lay bleeding his last and the woman was sobbing silently. Sam used his Colt to bludgeon the man closest to him as the other looked at him with a stupid expression on his face.

The older women held the young girl rocking her to and fro and rubbing her back as the girl sobbed. She was 'damaged goods' now and would find life very difficult from this point forward. The prisoners were forced to dig a grave and inter the dead Mexican father. At Captain Walker's direction the felon's hands were bound and the three roped into a string. The Rangers left the sobbing woman and her daughter as they rode back to their headquarters. The men would be turned over to the Judge Advocate's Office for confinement and trial by Courts-martial.

"Why so glum, Wally?" Sam asked. "You've seen this sort of thing before."

Sergeant Wally Carson thought silently for some time before he replied. "I was there at that ranch down on the Brazos when renegades butchered the entire family. I guess they raped the girls before they killed them but this is somehow different!"

"These men would have killed the women too if we hadn't interrupted their fun." Captain Walker pointed out the obvious. "It might have been better for the girl if they had. Let's get this bunch of slime back to the General and let him decide their fate."

The Ranger's rode in silence as Wally gave sharp tugs on the rope to make the prisoner's trip uncomfortable. It took several hours for the Rangers to retrace their route to General Taylor's Command. The humbled prisoners stood silently awaiting their fate.

"Turn them over to the Provost to await Courts-martial. Colonel Bliss, prepare General Courts-martial papers." General Taylor would have his chance to make an example of the criminals.

SIXTEEN

Colonel Bliss collected the names of the felons for the Court.

"Sergeant John J. Adams of Company 'I' 5th Infantry." The first man answered.

"Private William Radfield also of Company 'I' 5th Infantry. Said the second man.

"Private Peter Murphy of 'I' company also." The third man answered in a thick Irish brogue.

The prisoners were turned over to the Provost Marshall to be held in close confinement until the next day when the General Courts-martial could be convened. The Court was composed of Colonel Harney as President of the Court, Captain Bragg, Lieutenant P.T. Beauregard, Lieutenant U. S. Grant and Captain Merrill.

The proceeding was short as Captain Walker and Sergeant Carson testified to their knowledge of the crimes committed.

"The prisoners will rise to hear the sentence." Colonel Harney ordered.

The men rose and faced the court. They seemed apprehensive as the sentence was handed down.

"Sergeant John J. Adams, you have been found guilty of robbery and murder by this court. You will be reduced to the rank of private and fined one month's pay."

"Private William Radfield, You are also found guilty and are sentenced to 10 days imprisonment on bread and water and forfeiture of one month's pay."

"Private Peter Murphy, you are likewise guilty and are sentenced to death by firing squad which will be administered by your fellows of Company 'I' of the fifth infantry.

The unfortunate Murphy, the only foreign-born prisoner had received the harshest sentence.

"This Court-martial is adjourned. The sentencing documents will be forwarded to the Commanding General for appeal and review." Colonel Harney grinned.

Sergeant Adams returned to his unit as a private. He would suffer much harassment by the men he once commanded. Private Radfield was returned to the stockade to begin his 10 day sentence of piss and punk for a diet. One cup of water and a slice of stale bread would be his ration for each day of confinement. Peter Murphy, the only immigrant of the three, was held pending General Taylor's review of the case.

Colonel William 'perfect' Bliss had already read the sentencing document before passing it to the General. "It seems so unfair! Murphy gets a firing squad of his peers and the others get a slap on the wrist. What kind of message does that send to our troops?"

"Precisely the message I wish to convey. That all lapses of discipline will be harshly dealt with and the penalty can be severe!" General Taylor told his aide.

"Sir, this may increase the desertion rate among the foreign born troops." Bliss said.

"It very well may. It should decrease these incidents of troops raiding and pillaging among the civilian populace. We want their cooperation or at least their forbearance as we advance further into Mexico." General Taylor explained. "Order the sentences carried out and endorse the order."

Later in the day the entire 'I' Company was drawn up in parade on the execution spot. Ten riflemen stood waiting as Private Murphy was led to the stake where he was bound. A Catholic priest stood with the convicted man giving absolution. The priest sadly left Murphy as the Squad Leader offered the condemned man a blindfold which he refused.

"Ready, Aim, Fire!" The command was given and the unfortunate Irishman slumped at the stake. A doctor pronounced the man dead and his executioners cut him down. They were also to bury him.

Resentment ran rampant among the foreign troops at the uneven sentences of the offenders. All of the hardened troops felt that the three soldiers deserved to be punished but could not help notice that the Irishman had received the harshest punishment. Resentment simmered and festered until it finally came to a head as the carbuncle ripened and finally burst.

One of the most hated and harshest of Nativist Officers was Captain Braxton Bragg of the Flying Batteries. His victims waited their chance for revenge and finally took it. A large explosion was heard at the officer's test area. Many soldiers rushed toward the area where they discovered Captain Bragg covered with debris and wearing soot stains from the gunpowder covering his face. It was later determined that a six pound shell's fuse had been lit and the cannonball rolled into the tent where Bragg was soundly sleeping. Many were astonished at the Captain's survival. The purpose of the attempt on Bragg's life had the unexpected result that he doubled he harsh treatment of the foreign born under his command. The slightest offense, real or imaginary, received prompt punishment.

The Nativist Officer's continued to punish their foreign soldiers more harshly than the native born soldiers. Any German, French or even British offender suffered the horse, buck and gag and hanging by the thumbs. The native born American's weren't punished as harshly. This led to more desertions by the Irish especially, but Germans and other foreign born soldiers who were fed up with the unfair treatment by the officers and went over to the enemy in large numbers. The punishments meted out were in accordance with the Articles of War and the soldiery agreed with the need to punish offenders but resented being treated worse than their native born tent mates.

The soldiers continued training and no unit put more hours into that activity than the Artillery. Captain Washington's men were practicing moving a gun from a muddy hole when a soldier slipped and fell breaking his collar bone. He reported to his Captain and requested to see the surgeon.

"You god dammed Dutchie, if you go anywhere a medical tent I'll have you bucked and gagged and you'll spend all day in fetters." Captain Washington of Battery D of the flying artillery shouted. That night the unfortunate soldier Henry Ockter deserted.

"Good riddance!" Captain Washington replied when informed of the desertion of the German Soldier. "If I ever see him again, I'll hang him!"

The Captain would see the German again from the wrong side of John Reilly's battery in another battle.

SEVENTEEN

Training continued every day but Sunday until General Taylor moved his small Army south to confront General Santa Anna and the Mexican Army. The American Army followed the road to Saltillo and arrived at Agua Nueve where they rested. General Winfred Scott had siphoned off most of Tailor's Army and he was left with a thousand regulars and three thousand volunteers.

The Mexican Army continued their grueling march for Agua Nueve and was some fifteen miles away from the prize when a column of smoke rose in the sky. The Americans were retreating north. The fire was the American Army burning the food supplies.

General Taylor had withdrawn from the town and moved his men to the narrows, a forty foot pass through the mountains. The natural bottleneck would be very expensive to wrest from the American forces. The battle of Buena Vista began as the Mexican Army advanced into the narrows. The Mexicans called the place Angostura and the Americans knew it as Buena Vista after the name of the ranch property located there.

The Mexican Army passed through the lesser mountains and drew up on the wide plane that sloped uphill towards the American position at the narrows. Once through the narrows the ground widened out into another flat valley.

Colonel Morales and John Reilly rode in search of a site to mount his guns. A tall escarpment overlooked the field and would be a perfect spot to enfilade the American line at the narrows of Angostura.

"Have the men drag those cannon up here to the bluff." Colonel Morales ordered. "Notice that you will be able to bring you barrels to bear on every part of the battlefield while the Yankees will not be able to fire on your guns."

A wide valley lay between the Mexican troops and the narrows fortified by the Americans. Taylor deployed his forces to both side of the narrows of Angostura and sent his flying artillery under Bragg and Duncan to the mouth of the opening. The battle would be lopsided when it came. Taylor had less than six thousand troops facing Santa Anna's force of twenty five thousand.

The Mexicans advanced and the flying batteries raced out to five hundred yards in front of the American Infantry. They double-shot their guns with canister and fired on the Mexican advance. Reilly opened fire on the Americans from the bluff with his larger guns. He destroyed the flying batteries.

Captain John Paul Jones O'Brien's battery was almost annihilated as the infantry rushed forward and captured the guns. Mexican soldiers dragged the light six pounders from the field and returned them to their rear.

Jefferson Davis Mississippians arrived on the field and drove the Mexican Infantry back to their own lines. The field lay covered with the dead and dying from both forces. Their numbers were so great that the medical personnel could not care for them all. Many died awaiting care. Thick smoke from all the guns covered the field and smoke from a brushfire added to the cloud. The battle ended with night fall. Santa Anna withdrew to his original position and the troops built cooking fires. Both side rested.

The fires died down and the night waned as Captain Sam Walker and his Rangers set off on the scouting mission that General Taylor had requested. The first rays on the new sun appeared as the Rangers rode into Santa Anna's camp. The Mexican force had departed on a night march taking Taylor's light gun captured the day before with them.

"You are absolutely certain of what you report?" An incredulous General Taylor asked his Ranger.

"Yes General, Santa Anna stole a march in the night. He left the fires burning to deceive our men. He is in full retreat." Sam replied.

"But why? He certainly wasn't defeated. His force still outnumbered ours be five to one." The General wondered.

"General, one of the stragglers we captured seemed to think that Santa Anna is rushing to the port of Veracruz in order to prevent General Scott from taking that port." Sam said.

"Maybe this has some bearing on the matter." Old Rough and Ready held dispatches that he had just begun to read when the Ranger arrived. "Sound Officer Call!" Taylor ordered.

"I have been ordered to send the greater part of my command to Tampico where they will join with General Scott's force in preparation for an assault on Veracruz. I will remain here with about a thousand troops to pacify this part of Mexico. It seems that Mister Polk wishes to isolate me so that I cannot achieve any further victories." General Taylor said peevishly.

On the following day the troops that were assigned to General Scott's force were drawn up in parade formation. They passed in front of Old Rough and Ready as he took their salute and returned it with one of his own. His war was over. President Polk feared that Taylor would run for his office and attempted to isolate the General. It did not work. A month later General Taylor, the Hero of Buena Vista turned over his command and began the long journey back to Washington. He had resigned his commission and when he arrived in Washington he threw his hat into the ring. He ran for President against Polk who had feared that very thing.

The two men hated each other. They were from opposite sides of the political landscape but the hatred was more a personal matter. The President was the first one of his office that interfered with the Generals in the field. He dictated military policy. Polk had no military experience and tried to direct the war from a distance of almost three-thousand miles. General Taylor resented this attempt to usurp command.

The two men would meet on the political battlefield in the fall. In the interim General Taylor, the Hero of Buena Vista, was received with parades and awards. Congress voted him the prestigious ceremonial sword.

EIGHTEEN

Colonel Hays and the Texas Rangers rode in the van of the army making its way toward Tampico to join General Winfred Scott's Army. The regular cavalry had been assigned the skirmish duties and this left the Rangers to leisurely ride at a pace set by the Infantry.

"Colonel, what have you heard about this new General? What sort is he?" Sam asked his leader.

Colonel Hays thought for a minute before answering Sam's question. "I knew him when we were both a lot younger. He is a stickler for regulations! Some of his fellow officers call him 'old fuss and feathers' but not to his face. He is tough but fair. He'll be good in this job."

"Well he better be! Rumor has it that Santa Anna has already raised a force of fifty thousand men." Sam said.

"Well that may be, but he is very wasteful of his resources. He forces his men to march thirty miles a day and hardly feeds them. Many times he refuses to allow them to fill their canteens. Those Mexican soldiers are the best in the world and only their leadership is lacking. Under competent leaders they would surely defeat our force. We are always outnumbered by three or more to one." Colonel Hays explained.

"Then I suppose we have to be thankful that Pedro didn't shoot that rascal Santa Anna at Rio San Jacinto." Sam laughed. "No telling who would command the Mexican Army. Perhaps someone of some competency who would make good use of those campensinos."

"The casualty's figures show how lopsided the battle really was. Santa Anna lost four of five soldiers compared to our loses." Colonel Hays said. "Santa Anna ordered his men to advance into the mouths of our cannon without regard for his losses. Our defense of the narrows was impossible to breach in a frontal assault. He wasted his troops and then withdrew before the battle was decided. I'm afraid that the Mexican General was our greatest ally in the battle for the narrows."

"I don't understand why he didn't try to outflank us. That gully off to the east was a possible route to our rear. Taylor failed to defend it since he thought it an impossible route of advance for the Mexican Infantry." Sam replied.

"If it had been my command I would have infiltrated my troops under cover of darkness and sprung the trap at first light before the soldiers were fully awake." Colonel Hays said.

They rode in silence for a while until they reached a point where the road rose slightly and there they spied a rider racing his mount towards them. It was Sergeant Wally Carson. The Sergeant stopped in front of the two officers.

"You'll have to see this, sir, another massacre." Wally reported.

All three of the Rangers rode forward until they came to a farmhouse. The ruins were burning brightly indicating that the fire was of recent origin. Four dead lay scattered around the yard. The youngest victim was about ten years old. He had been shot in the back as he ran away.

"Colonel Hays, this couldn't have been any of the troops! They have been on the march all day." Sam said.

"No, I believe that the bandit Dominguez and his band of cutthroats are probably responsible. They are the only ones able to slip away long enough to commit such a deed."

"Suppose I detail a few of my men to shadow that slimy bastard?" Sam asked.

"That's an excellent idea Sam." Colonel Hays agreed. "But chose your men carefully. They'll have to be savvy enough to creep up on a sidewinder and catch him unawares."

Sam turned to Sergeant Wally Carson and said; "Wally, think you can do that?"

"Why certainly!" Wally replied. "It'll take at least a dozen men or more if we are to cover his actions day and night."

"I'll leave it to you then. Set up the operation and be sure you report in after each shift. I don't want anybody hurt. You are in charge and I hope you can catch him in the act. Use your own discretion."

The column continued its march for two more days before another incident occurred. This time the circumstances were quite different. The residents of the farmhouse had been successful in defending themselves. Sergeant Wally Carson and five other Rangers arrived at the scene as the attackers were crawling undercover for the house. The Rangers charged the bandits who fled leaving one man dead.

"You know these men?" Wally asked the Mexican ranchero.

"Si, Senor, he is one of the banditos that ride with Cicatriz. They are very bad men. The Mexican army has been trying to catch him for some time. Now that the army has gone he has become much bolder with his raiding and pillaging."

"Where do you suppose he will hit next?" Sam asked.

"One said that they were going to raid the Rancho Archelitta about five miles over there. General Santa Anna took most of the men with him to Mexico, the Capitol."

"Hernandez, ride back and get the rest of the boys. We are probably going to need them. They have a large band and it might take a few more men." Wally ordered.

When Wally and his men arrived at the ranch the bandits had already begun their assault on the main house. Its occupants had barricaded themselves and were returning fire on the bandit gang. About half of the attackers were armed with firearms and the rest carried knives and machetes. They moved from cover to cover using any shield to protect them from the firing of the house occupants.

Wally coordinated his attack with the next rush for cover by the bandits. He spurred his mount forward as did all the other Rangers at the same time firing his Colts to break their resolve. Several bandits went down and one tried to slip away. Wally rode him down. The entire action took only seconds. Wally leaped from his horse and disarmed the bandit. It was the leader of the pack of outlaws, Cicatriz. One look at the man's face confirmed Wally's suspicion. A large scar ran across his cheek turning his continence into an ugly map of the cruelty hidden within the man.

An old man, now sure it was safe to come out, left the house and approached Wally. "Muchos Gracias, Senor. We thought we were dead. He is a very bad man and has killed many. What will you do to him?"

"That's up to the Colonel, but, I imagine we have a trial and hang him." Wally told the old man.

NINETEEN

Colonel Hays and Sam Walker arrived on scene as they spoke. "What have we here, Sergeant?"

Wally explained that they had arrived as the banditos had been raiding the ranch and they had disarmed the felons and killed several of their number.

"That seems an excellent spot." Colonel Hays pointed to an ancient tree with a sturdy lower branch. "You've been found guilty of murder, robbery and disturbing the peace. How do you plead?"

Most of the bandits stood stoically by as the Rangers rounded up their horses and bound their hands behind their backs. Their leader, Cicatriz babbled his innocence. He was crying as the Rangers hoisted him onto his horse and led him to the tree. A ranger stood behind each horse and on the Colonel's nod whipped the horse forward. The felons kicked and tried to scream but it was over in a few moments.

"They'll not be bothering you again." The Colonel said to the smiling old man.

The Rangers rode back to the column except for Wally and his patrol. He and his men would continue riding patrol until they were relieved by the night patrol. The day passed with no further incidents. They left the bandit's horses with the surprised and grateful ranch owner and patrolled ever further down the road.

The column rode towards the sleepy little fishing village called 'Maderno Tampico' which was over a hundred miles south of the mouth of the Rio Grande. No Mexican force opposed their landing. General Winfred Scott had been gathering units of the U.S. Army in preparation for the seaborne invasion of Veracruz much further down the coast.

The General received the advance party of troops of General Taylor's Command.

Colonel Hays and Captain Walker were the first to arrive at Tampico and sought out the new Commander of American troops who had already established his headquarters of the Army of Occupation.

"What is your situation?" General Scott asked of the Texans.

"We rode in to report to you Sir. The Army is advancing smartly and the lead elements will arrive later this day." Colonel Hays told the General.

"Did you see any action on the march, any sign of the enemy?" Scott inquired.

"Only some minor banditry activity. My Rangers neutralized them." Colonel Hays reported.

"Did Colonel Bliss come with the troops?" Scott asked.

"He is in the van and should be here in a few hours." Hays replied.

"Have him report to me as soon as he arrives. I shall need his assistance in organizing this mess." General Scott waved his hand over the hodgepodge of men and equipment scattered over the landscape.

Sam Walker and his men selected an area just outside of the town and began to establish a bivouac site. They had just finished setting up their area when the first of the column arrived. Colonel Bliss rode with the General Officers and Sam informed them that Scott was waiting for them.

"William, what a pleasure seeing you again. I urgently require your help organizing this mess." General Scott said with a showing of genuine affection. Colonel Bliss was family having married Scott's eldest daughter some years previously.

"You've served together before this?" General Twiggs asked.

"Oh, yes Colonel Bliss and I served together many times and he is the best Adjutant I ever had under my command." Scott replied.

The officers went off to see to their troops. Tomorrow they would plan for the invasion of Veracruz, today they would settle into bivouac. Guards would be posted and roving patrols by the Rangers on the outskirts of the camp would search for deserters.

The long night had passed and the first light of the new day shone on the horizon as the first villagers trickled into with their goods. The market square began to fill as more farmers arrived with crops to be sold in the market place.

After breakfast General Scott ordered that Officer's Call be sounded. The Commanding Officers arrived at Scott's headquarters ready to begin the plans for the conquest of Veracruz. To seaward lay a huge fleet of every sort of vessel. Naval gunships lay anchored next to shallow draft coastal schooners.

"Gentlemen, I give you the city of Veracruz. How may we attack and take it with the fewest losses?" General Scott addressed the assembled officers.

The assembly discussed the situation for many minutes before a suggestion was made to attack south of the city and neutralize its outer defenses.

"Where would you we suggest we land the men?" General Scott asked.

"Here, about five miles south of the city!" General Twiggs said. "The ground is mostly sand dunes. We could supplement our artillery with some of the heavier guns from the Navy's gunships in order to lay siege to the city."

"General, I think we need more accurate information about the area. What I propose is that we send a small patrol behind enemy lines to discover their layout." Colonel Hays suggested.

"A reconnaissance to discover his troop dispositions would seem in order." General Scott agreed. "How do you propose to accomplish that, Colonel Hays?"

"See this small town, Diablado, about ten miles south of Veracruz? It seems to be a fishing village and will have a small dock for the fishing fleet. I suggest we send several men to unload the horses and skirt the enemy positions. My men are an obvious choice for the mission and they speak Mexican so they would understand what was said." Colonel Hays suggested.

"Who would you send on such a dangerous mission?" Scott asked.

"Sam Walker here and Wally and Pedro. They can leave immediately if that is ok." Hays said.

"Colonel Bliss, please select the proper vessel and have the hostlers load the men and horses so that they can depart on the tide." General Scott ordered.

TWENTY

As the Texas Rangers boarded the vessel for the long voyage to Diablado the Armies of the 'Immortal Three-fourths' as Santa Anna was sometimes called, rode into Veracruz to a hero's welcome. The title was in reference to the leg he had lost in the 1812 battle with the French Army. It had been an astonishing victory for the Mexicans and helped to establish Santa Anna as a true Mexican Hero.

Traces of his former beauty were still evident in his craggy features at middle age. He was always impeccably attired and sat his horse ramrod straight. He looked the part of a General Officer. He was a vain man who carried many titles, most of his own choosing. His Army consisted of a cadre on professional soldiers while the most men consisting of conscripts. His soldiers were capable of impressive soldiering skills and were to take on incredible hardships. His leadership had proved lacking over the years but his fearlessness in battle was legendary in the Mexican forces. Now he would have to use those forces to defend Veracruz.

Santa Anna deployed most of his Infantry in the town. His heavy artillery he sited south of the town in the sand dunes where he thought the main invasion force would attack. The lighter guns were deployed north of town. He planned to make the Yankees pay for the invasion of his home town. Santa Anna owned a large plantation not far from Veracruz. His preparations complete, Santa Anna sank into to a life of debauchery with several beautiful courtesans in the nicest abode in town. He left it for his subordinates to conduct day-to-day operations. He would wait. General Torrejon's cavalry provided a screen of roving mounted patrols encircling the city. The situation was quiet until a rider arrived at Santa Anna's HQ with unsettling news. Mexico City was being torn apart by riots and demonstrations against the war. The Catholic Church and the large landholders were behind the plot. Santa Anna hurried to Mexico to quell the riots.

Sam Walker, his Sergeant Carson and Pedro the Texas Rangers watched as the Quartermaster's men loaded their mounts onto the coastal steamer. They would sail on the next tide for the fishing village of Diablado. Several days later they tied up to an excellent wharf. A gangplank was run out and the Rangers walked the horses from the ship.

They rode to the livery stables and sought out the owner. He was a short dark Mexican with a ready smile who offered them lunch. After feeding the horses he conducted them to a table in the yard and summoned his wife to prepare lunch. The Texans spoke Mexican fluently and soon realized that the livery owner thought them to be Mexican. Conversation soon focused on the War.

"The Napoleon of the West as Santa Anna calls himself has been a disaster for Mexico. He passed a law allowing him to force the Church and large land owners to pay for his war." The owner said.

"We heard that there was widespread rioting in the Capitol." Pedro replied.

"Yes, I'd heard that too. The civilian population is being incited by the Church to rebel and throw out the Great Santa Anna but the people still support him. Quien Sabe?" The man called Juan said.

"And the army, are they not about the countryside?" Sam asked.

"No, Senor. Every available soldier is gathered at Veracruz where the Yankees will attack." Juan replied.

"How can you be sure?" Sam questioned.

"Santa Anna's men captured dispatches from the Americano General with the plans of an invasion at that place." Juan replied.

"So, Santa Anna stands ready to repel this supposed invasion?" Sam asked.

"Si, Senor. He is ready! He commands twenty-five thousand troops including some of the best. I fought with him in the Pastry War. That's where he lost his leg. He even had a state funeral for the leg!" Juan informed them.

"So that is where he learned the craft of war!" Sam said.

"Santa Anna had been in the army his entire life except for the three times he served as Presidente of Mexico. He was deposed and sent into exile and now he had returned and is President once more." The livery owner explained.

"We had better ride while we still have some daylight left." Pedro suggested.

They thanked the Mexican and Sam paid him with a Spanish silver dollar. He had wisely thought ahead and carried only Spanish coin. The Mexican took the silver coin and pointed out that it was far too great an amount of money for his services.

"Da nada." Sam said.

"You think he is convinced that we are what we say we are?" Wally asked.

"He suspects nothing!" Sam said.

The Texas Rangers rode though the dusty streets of the small town and soon gained the open countryside. They were easy in the saddle that came from years of hard riding. Their route took them far inland to avoid patrols that were securing the Mexican Army's rear. They found a spot to stay the night. It was a small hill with only one tree at the top. They knew from past experience not to camp under the tree and stretched out their bedrolls some distance from it. If they were disturbed during the night they would be in a better position to stave off an attack by any intruders. Each Texas Ranger stood watch through the night which passed uneventfully.

The morning sun was just rising into the sky as the Ranger enjoyed their morning coffee. "What's the plan, Captain?" Wally asked. He had been wondering how they would be able to reconnoiter the Mexican troop dispositions and escape unharmed to report back to Scott.

Sam was rifling through he duffle looking for some items which he handed to Pedro. The first thing he found was an ugly sombrero which was very dirty and bore now of the fancy decorations so common to the Mexican headgear. The other item was a serape of muted tones. "Put them on." Sam said. "But first give me your Colts. They would give you away if the Mexicans discover you in their lines."

"You want me to go into the Mexican lines alone without my arms?" Pedro asked.

"Yes." Sam said. "Your story is that you're a vaquero searching for your lost cattle. Think that will work if you're stopped? Here." Sam offered Pedro an ancient horse pistol such as a cowboy would have in his possession.

"I can make that work but where will you and Wally be while I'm scouting out their line?" Pedro asked.

"We'll ride well south of the Mexican positions to discover a suitable landing beach. After we find such a beach we will return and wait for you here." Sam replied.

"You don't think my horse will give me away?" Pedro asked.

"No. It's just the sort of mount that a vaquero would ride. Tell them that you're on a cattle drive to Veracruz to sell beef to Santa Anna. That should allay suspicions and set their moths to watering. I hear that Santa Anna isn't a very good feeder." Sam laughed.

"Via con Dios." Sam said as Pedro nudged his horse in the direction of Veracruz.

Pedro rode for about an hour before he was challenged.

"Halt! Who goes there?" The Mexican rifleman asked as he leveled his musket at the Ranger.

Pedro related his cover story to the sentry and was pleased when the sentry accepted it. "Passar Senor." The sentry waved his hand in a grand gesture in the direction of the town.

TWENTY-ONE

The Ranger rode slowly through the town without being challenged again. He discovered that the town was more lightly defended in the north than in the south. He found the field artillery to the south and carefully noted the position of each gun. Finally satisfied that there was nothing further to be learned, he retraced his route to the meeting place. He had coffee brewing when the other two Rangers returned to the camp site.

"What did you find in the city?" Sam asked Pedro as he handed him his belongings.

Pedro buckled on his guns and replaced the ugly Mexican hat with his own Stetson hat before he replied. He sketched out the troop dispositions, along with the field pieces and Sam was satisfied they were in possession of the latest intelligence about the Mexican Army's defenses. Sam told Pedro of his results.

"The landing beach is about two and a half miles from the forward Mexican lines. It is well suited for a seaborne invasion. There is even a babbling brook for fresh water right there. I think General Scott will be pleased with our reconnaissance." Sam smiled. "We still have two days before the boat arrives. We'll take our time getting back and only arrive at the livery the day before the boat arrives."

The Rangers rode due west until they discovered a wooded area where they set up camp. They built a fire and settled in for the night. Their campsite was far enough away from the road to shield them from prying eyes. The night passed quietly.

The sun was high in the sky when Wally pointed to the road. They crawled to the edge of the wood and looked out at the road. A company of cavalry rode leisurely to the north. They seemed in no hurry as if they had all day.

"Impress gang." Sam mouthed. Torrejon's horsemen were raiding the villages for recruits who they conscripted into Santa Anna's Army. They were to be given very little training and obsolete arms before being forced into the breach.

The Rangers waited in the woods almost the entire day before the cavalry troop returned. As they passed the spot where the Rangers waited they noticed something had been added to the patrol. Two lines of men and boys walked between the horsemen. These were the conscripts taken without their consent from surrounding villages.

"Poor bastards." Wally said. "Most of them have no idea what this war is about and, at the first shot, will turn and run back to their villages."

"Yeah,' Sam agreed, 'Those that are not killed or maimed by the first volley."

The Rangers kept a cold camp that night. It would not be very good were they to be discovered before they had the chance to report their findings to the General. The night passed without incident and they were up at first light preparing for the trip back to Diabaldo. A disturbance in the woods caused them to be instantly on the alert. A small sound came from the trees to the south. The Rangers spread out and sought the source of the noise.

"Don't shoot, Senor!" A young Mexican shouted. He was about fifteen years old and not a menace to the Rangers.

"Who are you and what are you about?" Sam asked not unkindly.

"I am Francisco from the village of Diablado. Santa Anna's men raided the town and took all the men and boys for their army. I escaped." The young Mexican explained his presence in the wood.

"We are going there now. Have you eaten this day?" Wally asked.

"No, Senor. I have been hiding from the soldiers." Francisco replied.

Wally shoved the remains of breakfast at the young man. "Eat!" He said.

They traveled for some time out of sight of the road until Francisco motioned for them to follow him. He led them to faint trail on the opposite side of the road which led up a slight rise. He pointed below to where the village of Diablado lay. "There." He said.

The shortcut saved them several miles of travel and they soon reached the outskirts of the town. Sam rode ahead to make sure it was safe to proceed. He waved the others on and they were soon at the livery stables. The owner of the stables rushed forward and embraced the young man.

"Francisco, how did you get away?" Juan asked. "But come. I forget my manners."

They sat at the table in the courtyard of the livery. Francisco described his escape from his captures. He had hidden in a ditch when they had stopped to rest and when the Cavalry had gone, he blundered into the same woods where he'd met the Rangers. Mamacito had prepared a lunch of frijoles and chili's.

Sam made arrangements to leave their horses in the care of the stable owner. Pedro went to prepare the signal fire on a high hill to signal the coaster to put into port. Then they settled down to wait for nightfall. When it was completely dark Pedro slipped away and lit the signal fire. The Rangers accompanied by father and son strode down to the dock. The longboat from the coaster was awaiting them.

The Captain welcomed the Rangers aboard his vessel. "Everything go according to plan?" He asked.

Sam informed the Captain that they had left the horses and that this port would be the landing point for the horsemen. "It's the perfect place to unload the cavalry's animals."

The trip was uneventful and the Rangers found that the Generals were anxiously awaiting their return. After a pleasant voyage they docked at Tampico. Colonel Hays met the boat and greeted his Rangers when they disembarked.

"How successful were you in scouting out the enemy's formations?" He asked Sam.

"Pretty successful. Let's report to the General and tell him what we discovered.

TWENTY-TWO

General Scott and his adjutant were alone when they arrived. They briefed these officers and then Sam suggested the fishing port as a point for the horsemen to disembark. "We even led our horses down the gang plank. Another thing you might consider is unshipping some of your heavier guns onto barges for the trip ashore. You are sure to need them when it's time to breach the walls of the city."

"We had considered that and have procured three flat-bottomed scows for the job." General Scott replied.

Scott was immensely pleased with the Ranger's report.

"We leave on the morning tide. Go get some rest. Colonel Bliss, sound Officer's Call."

Colonel Hays summoned Sam to his quarters. "Sam, I want you and your men to go into the port in advance of the other horsemen. Secure the docks so that we can offload the horses without incident."

"Shall I take the entire company? You're not expecting a welcoming committee?" Sam asked.

"One can't be too careful." Colonel Hay replied.

The small vessel that carried the Rangers to the port of Diablado approached the dock. Sam and his two men had slipped off the boat earlier and retrieved their mounts. They sat waiting as the others led their mounts down the gangplank. It wasn't long before a dozen more Rangers ringed the wharf in a tight security screen. In a very short time the remainder of the Ranger Company was offloaded and the Cavalry began unloading their horses. Colonel Hays arrived with the last men. They now numbered 150 of the finest horse soldiers available and would be able to trounce any enemy that challenged them.

"Sam, let's get up in the high country so as to avoid the enemy security screen." The Colonel said as he motioned for Sam to lead the way.

The small force rode due west away from the ocean and into the tree line. They stopped a distance from the main road where Sam had seen Torrejon's Cavalry on his previous trip. Screened from the road by the trees they turned south to ride around the city. The outriders located some cavalry resting on the road and steered the column of horsemen around the obstacle. Silence was the order of the day and only the creaking of saddles gave them away but no one was close enough to hear. They finally came to a position behind the dune below the city. Scouts saw the Mexican cavalry picketed uphill from the beach guns. The 24 and 28 pound guns were in the perfect spot to enfilade the landing.

Two and a half miles to the south sweating American soldiers and sailors manhandled naval cannon removed from the warships into position. The Infantry was assembled with the United States Marines in the lead. Lieutenant Gillespie led one company of Marines into battle. When the Mexican forces learned they were under attack they began firing their heavy cannon at the landing force. For some unknown reason they only fired solid shot which cost few causalities among the American Infantry. The American Artillery returned the Mexican fire with canister and grapeshot. This took a terrible toll on the Mexican Infantry guarding the cannon.

Lieutenant Gillespie understanding the situation rose up and drew his sword. "Charge!" He shouted and his company followed him into the breach of the large cannon. The sight of the Marines charging with fixed bayonets gleaming in the sunlight unnerved the Mexican gunners and they quickly began to flee in the direction of the city.

General Anastisio Torrejon's Cavalry raced into the fray to stem the rout but was surprised to find horsemen in their rear. Colonel Hays and his Rangers along with the Regular cavalry had waited for the moment and broke over his rear. Terrejon and his force had no choice but to run away in the direction of Veracruz. It was a total rout for the Mexican force outside the walls of the city.

"I guess that'll learn them." Pedro said as they rode up to Colonel Hays. "We captured a dozen prisoners, Colonel, what shall we do with them?"

"Take their parole and return them to the Mexicans." Colonel Hays directed.

Sam rode up with a Marine Lieutenant and stopped in front of Colonel Hays. "Colonel this is Lieutenant Gillispie of the Marines. He thinks we may be able to get those guns back into action against the city walls."

"The Mexican Artillerist left much solid shot which is just the thing to batter down those walls but what I require is help in placing them in battery. Perhaps your horsemen could help?" The Marine asked.

"Sam do what it takes, help the man out." Colonel Hays ordered.

The guns were horsed into position to bring a fire upon the city walls and in less than an hour the boom of the cannon echoed across the battlefield. All of the Mexican Army outside the wall sought sanctuary within the city. Now the siege of Veracruz began. General Scott had captured the national road to the west and began shelling Veracruz. Scotts Quartermaster, U. S. Grant was busy buying mules from the countryside. Day and night the cannon roared and shell after shell fell on the populace for several days. The Marines and Rangers forced their way into the city through an opening created by the cannon fire.

The day was passing into evening when a white flag appeared on the rampart. The Mexicans were seeking a truce. The order was passed to cease fire and Colonel Hays rode out to meet a Mexican Officer who also bore a white flag.

"What is it that you wish?" Colonel Hays asked.

"My General wishes to beg for surrender terms." The Mexican Officer said.

Colonel Hays rode to Scott's HQ and reported his encounter with the Mexican.

"Tell him that they will surrender their arms, their stores and their colors in the morning and then they will be permitted to leave." General Scott said. "Convey those demands and in the mean time we will order a ceasefire."

Colonel Hays did as ordered. The Mexican returned to the city and before the last shot echoed across the battlefield he was back. The Mexicans had agreed to the terms. The battle for Veracruz was over. The Americans had suffered 28 killed and a few more wounded. The Mexicans lost over two hundred civilians killed in the bombardment and twice that number of soldiers.

At nine the next day the Mexican Army stacked their arms and laid out their colors as the Mexican General offered General Scott his sword. General Scott allowed the Officer to keep the weapon. The Mexican Army formed ranks and began the long march west.

"God! They've three times our number, why did they surrender?" Sam asked.

"An Army is only as good as its leader." Colonel Hays replied.

TWENTY-THREE

The Americans did not tarry. The very next day they began the next phase of the march on the Capitol. They had suffered few combat casualties but left over a thousand men behind suffering from 'el vomito' as yellow fever was known in Mexico. Scott wanted to get his force out of the fever zone as quickly as possible. His destination was Jalapa, a city some four-thousand feet above the zone of pestilence and seventy five miles west on the National Road.

Unencumbered with equipment the Mexican Army from Veracruz had made good time and was over a day ahead of the Americans. Both forces were striving for the same destination. Desertions continued to plague both armies as Mexican Infantry, mainly conscripts made for their homes. Foreigners, mostly Irishmen, continued to leave the army at every chance.

Sam and his Rangers rode in front of the army to prevent any ambush and the Mexican spy company and the evil Dominguez rode skirmishers a mile to each side of the column. The weather was turning warm and the Texans shed outer layers of clothing. Summer was almost on them and the days were getting very warm. After days in the saddle they came at last to the pass called Cerro Gordo. At first glance the position seemed impregnable. General Scott thought so too.

"I wonder why they called it that." Wally asked.

"Never thought about it." Sam replied. "Cerro means hill in Spanish and Gordo means fat. So it's Fat Hill?' Sam laughed.

"It looks pretty awesome to me." Wally said.

"Never fear. Old Fuss and Feathers will come up with a plan!" Sam replied to Wally's fears.

General Scott convened a meeting of his Engineers. Major Robert E. Lee, Lieutenant P. T. Beauregard, Joe Johnson and Zealous B. Tower assembled at Scotts HQ. "Gentlemen I wish for you to take turns making night reconnaissance of a way around that dam pass. It is an impossible position to take by frontal assault and we must find a way around that obstacle!"

"I'll go see what I can find." Lieutenant Beauregard said.

"Go! Report back to me what you find out about a route." Major Lee ordered.

Lieutenant Beauregard searched and thought he knew a way around the Mexican Army. He had noticed a ravine to the south of the road and he took an enlisted man and rode out of camp. Pierre Beauregard had been gone for over an hour when he returned to report his findings.

"Well it seems a promising route. Have Sergeant William Smyth report to me and we shall go exploring." Major Lee ordered. "Bill Smyth is the best outdoorsman we have in the Engineers."

Lieutenant Beauregard took the two Engineers to the spot he had found. "This is the spot."

"Well, Lieutenant, how far did you go into the ravine?" Major Lee asked.

"Not far. We wanted to report our findings before we explored any further." The Lieutenant replied.

"We'll take it from here. Thank you." Lee dismissed Lieutenant Beauregard.

Lee pointed his head in the direction of travel and Smyth followed the Major. The two men cautiously climbed La Atalaya until they found a trail leading down and away from the hill. They heard voices coming from the hilltop speaking Spanish. Lee pointed to a faint path that led off in the distance. His Engineers could hack out a trail behind the enemy lines. The two men crawled through the underbrush until they came to a spring that spilled into a small lake.

Robert E. Lee was in the lead when they heard voices very close to where the stood. Lee turned to warn Smyth only to find him gone. He looked around for a place to hide and opted for a deadfall laying some distance from the lake. He crawled under the log and was immediately sorry. Ants and other insects made his existence unbearable.

The voices he had heard belonged to soldiers that had come to fill their canteens from the brook. Several of the Mexican soldiers came and sat on the log covering Lee. It seemed a lifetime before they left. Lee waited a lifetime before he heard something. Sergeant Smyth was whspering his name. He rolled from under the log scratching his insect bites. The Sergeant had gathered some plants that lined the creek. He broke the leaves and began dabbing the bites with the nectar. The relief was instantaneous!

"What is that?" Lee whispered.

"Aloe Vera grows wild all over Mexico." Smyth answered in a whisper.

Major Lee pointed to the trail the soldiers had come down. He led the way cautiously uphill. They reached the summit and were surprised to find themselves over a hundred yards behind the enemy position. Wordlessly Lee pointed back in the direction in which they had come. They had been gone for hours and General Scott fearing for their safety had dispatched Lieutenant Zealous Tower and a squad of riflemen to find them. "What kept you?" Tower asked.

"I'll explain it when we see the General." Major Lee his ranking officer said.

"We were having misgivings about you safety, Major" General Scott said. "What did you find?"

Major Lee explained the difficulties they had encountered. "We could cut a trail through that brush and come out a full hundred yards in their rear but I would need more men than I've got in my command to accomplish that task in one night."

"Send for Lieutenant Malone." General Scott asked his Adjutant Colonel Bliss.

When Mick Malone reported to General Scott he was informed that he was to accompany the Engineers and cut a trail through the brush around the enemy. "Sir, when do we attack?" Mick asked.

"At first light if the trail is ready. Warn the men to make as little noise as possible and have them get brush axes from the Engineers. If we are successful we will take Cerro Gordo before a new dawn arrives."

Major Lee briefed the troops on the night's operations. "The trail must be wide enough to bring the light artillery guns with us. Nothing disconcerts an enemy more that to receive fire from his rear. All set, let's go."

TWENTY-FOUR

They began the laborious task of hacking a road out of the wilderness. General Twiggs regulars and Colonel Jeff Davis' Mississippians Volunteers followed closely behind the Engineers who had almost gained the spring before they heard voices.

"Manolo. Did you hear that?" The Mexican soldier asked his friend.

"It's just the artillery preparing new positions for their guns. Who else would be chopping down trees at this hour?" The second Mexican responded.

The Artillery guns and the caissons made almost no noise and an hour before daybreak the American Army was in Position to assault the Mexican's rear. The cannon were hidden just below the military crest of the hill and the Infantry was hidden in the brush that grew to the crest of the hill. General Twiggs raised his sword and waved the Infantry forward. The men rose silently from cover and began marching to the enemy's rear. They had covered almost all the ground up to the Mexican positions before the alarm was raised. The enemy Infantry realized that all was lost and ran from the hill.

Sam Grant had quietly joined the assault troops and was manhandling the guns into battery. The guns began firing over the heads of the American troops and into the fleeing army. A grinning Sam Grant stood passing ammunitions to the gun crews. The Mexican Generals soon realized their predicament and ordered a retreat. Before the sun set the pass of Cerro Gordo it was in American hands and the Mexican Army was in full retreat. Casualties were light on both sides. General Scott was pleased. The Mexicans had abandoned all of the stores and most of their guns and were racing away from the pass.

The battle of Cerro Gordo was over and the Mexican Army was in full retreat for Jalapa. The road to the Capitol was open. Mexico lay two hundred miles west on the National Highway. The Americans had taken 3000 prisoners and over sixty cannon at a cost of 63 dead and 368 wounded. The quantities of materials and guns taken or abandoned was amazing. Cerro Gordo would be listed as a great American victory.

General Winfred Scott rested his army while the necessary tasks of burial and preparing the supplies for transport were seen to. Sam Grant, The Quartermaster was busy buying stock to move the captured supplies and guns. He had stripped the surrounding country of draft animals and finally had enough beasts to carry the overly large baggage train onward to Mexico.

The Rangers continued patrolling the countryside and incidents of robbery and murder were reported daily. Sam and his men were unable to close with the bandits. Then Wally Carson had an idea.

"There was another incident today." Wally told Sam. "We always seem to arrive on scene too late to catch the bandits. I've an idea. Suppose we circulate a rumor that a ranch further down the road is rich pickings?"

"Excellent idea! Then we could be in place when they attack." Sam agreed. "Let's do it."

The two Rangers searched for a likely target and soon found it. A small estancho lay about ten miles from their current local. Wally and Pedro began the rumor and soon the word was all over the camp. They waited a full day and then rode off as if on patrol.

Word of the fabricated tale reached the ears of Dominguez and he collected his gang of thieves and bandits. "We have a rich prize waiting for us just down this road. Here is what we must do." The bandit leader of the company of spies laid out his plan of attack. The rode out on patrol just after breakfast.

The Texas Rangers were hidden from sight as the bandit gang rode up to the hacienda where Pedro stood pretending to groom his horse. Dominguez slid from his horse and approached Pedro and began to ask him a question. At that moment a shot rang out. Pedro dived for cover and the bandits dispersed. The gun battle that followed lasted for some time. Dominguez leaped on his horse and raced for the cover of the trees. One by one the bandits fell to the Rangers fire until no one moved. Most of the Mexican bandits were dead and the few still living would die of their wounds in short order.

Dominguez had found a spot in the brush that afforded suitable cover and had withdrawn his strange rifle. He sighted on Sam Walker and slowly drew the trigger. Sam fell.

Wally had seen the muzzle blast of the sniper rifle and returned his fire. Without stopping to help his fallen commander he raced to the location from which the shot had come and rode over the bandit chief. Leaping from his mount as he drew his Colt 44 and aimed at Dominguez's head he shouted for his comrades. "Here!"

The Rangers rushed to the scene to find the bandit leader's hands bound behind his back. They dragged Dominguez back to the space before the farmhouse.

Sam sat up bleeding from a wound in his upper arm. Wally went to him and asked him his condition.

"How is it Sam?" Wally asked.

"Just a scratch. I'll be fine as soon as I get this tended to and we hang that bastard!" Sam replied.

Sam's wound was bandaged and he stood up and faced the bandit. "Any last words?"

Dominguez babbled something unintelligible as he was placed on his horse and a noose placed on his neck. He was led to a very large tree and the rope secured.

"No! I want to do it." Sam went to the rear of the horse and slapped him on the rump as the Mexican bandit screamed which was choked off as the noose snapped shut. Dominguez kicked and twisted as justice was served. He had been responsible for so much suffering that Sam took a twisted satisfaction at seeing him die.

They checked each of the bandits and found one man still alive. Wally calmly drew his Colt and placed a bullet between the man's eyes. It was done! Mexico would be a far safer place in future days.

Wide eyed residents of the ranch came out to view the results of the gun battle. Sam explained the situation and told them to strip and bury the dead bandits. He offered the horses and belongings to the ranchers. Satisfied with the day's work Sam ordered his Rangers to resume their patrol knowing that the atrocities would cease.

"And so the spy company no longer exists." Sam finished his report to Colonel Hays. "Will you inform the General?"

"No Sam, better to keep this among our little group. Instruct the men not to discuss it. The General will find out they are gone soon enough. In any rate, we've been ordered to march. We shall go to Jalapa tomorrow."

The Rangers, who were a closed-mouthed bunch at any rate, were told not to discuss the execution of the Mexican bandits. They were also informed that the column would depart the next day for the city of Jalapa.

TWENTY-FIVE

The American Army broke camp the next day and began the march to Jalapa. Word was received on the march that Santa Anna had declared Jalapa to be an open city. General Winfred Scott was relieved at this news. The city was seventy miles closer to the Capitol of Mexico and Scott could almost taste the eventual victory. The war would be over soon but much still remained to be accomplished.

The Archbishop and Mayor along with other dignitaries waited at the entrance to the town of Jalapa as General Scott rode at the head of the American column to where they waited.

"As you know, General Scott, Santa Anna has declared Jalapa and open city. We are here to welcome you and your men and extend our hospitality." The Archbishop stated formally. He wished to determine if the General would honor the open city designation Santa Anna had declared.

"Your Holiness,' General Scott replied 'My men have been instructed to respect civilian rights and property. Any infractions will be promptly dealt with by Court martial immediately."

Jalapa was an old city filled with Spanish architecture and was already two-hundred years since its founding. American troops were awed by the grandiose structures but the Catholic Cathedral was the finest old structure of them all. Civilians smiled at the soldiers as they made their way through the old town. Scott hoped there would be no incidents with the populace.

Sam and his Rangers were conducted to an old mansion that had once hosted Spanish Royalty. The rooms were very ornate, furnished with the finest furniture of old Spain, most of which had been imported from the old country. The rank and file of the Ranger Command pitched their tents about the grounds. Strange flowers and trees were just beginning to bloom and the fragrance filled the air. The building was of colonial origin and was massive in size. The Rangers would treasure their stay there.

Night patrols about the city were established and the other soldiers not on duty were free to roam the city. Sam and some of the other rangers strolled into the center of town and arrived at the central square. An open air restaurant beckoned them and they decided to eat their dinner at the open air part of the establishment. As the Texans dined on fine European style cuisine they watched the nightly parada of young people and the chaperones parading around the large open square. A band played soft Mexican love songs and the night air was heavy with the perfume of tropical vegetation. It was an enchanted evening and the Rangers ambled back to their quarters in an excellent mood. Sam sank into his fine, soft, feathered bed. He left the window open and drifted off to sleep with the sounds of the night birds filling his slumber.

"Corporal of the guard, Post number two!" The alarm disturbed Sam's sleep. He was instantly awake and hung his head out of the window. Where was the alarm issuing from? He hurriedly dressed and raced out of the bedroom. Several sentries held three men in captivity against the wall of the very next residence.

"What is happening, private?" Sam asked the guard who lifted a hand and pointed to a figure prone on the ground of the garden. "We caught these three in the act."

The Provost Marshall and his men arrived then and the Provost took charge of the situation. His men marched to suspects off to the guard house where they would be lodged until the morning. Sam returned to his bed.

Sam and Wally returned to the open air restaurant they had visited the night before. They were eating the first ham and farm-fresh eggs that they had in a long time when the messenger found them.

"Sir, General Scott would like to see you as soon as you're free." The young officer saluted and left.

"What's all this about?" Wally asked.

"I don't know. You might want to tag along and we'll find out." Sam replied.

The Texans went to the large building that housed the General's HQ. Sentries stopped them from entering. "Inform General Scott that Captain Walker and his Sergeant are reporting as ordered." Sam requested.

The tall distinguished General came to the door. "Captain Walker, I have need of your assistance. I understand that you were the first officer to reach the disturbance on last night?"

"I arrived moments before the Provost Marshall and found guards holding three suspects at bayonet point. A man was down on his face in the garden and since the Provost had the situation in hand, I went back to bed."

"How did you know what was occurring to arrive so quickly at the scene?" General Scott asked.

"I am billeted in the next house and heard the sentry call for the Corporal of the guard." Sam replied.

"Very well, I am convening a Court Martial for later in the day to try those men. You will be prepared to give testimony at that trial." Scott ordered.

Sam arrived at the place of Court Martial to give his testimony in the case. Colonel Harney was again the presiding officer.

Two of the offenders were men of Colonel Harney's Command and the others was from 'B' Company, 5th Infantry.

The trial was over quickly and Colonel Harney, the President of the Court pronounced the sentence.

"Sergeant Brady, you have been found guilty of murder and robbery and are hereby sentenced to fifty lashes of the cat, a reduction to the lowest enlisted rank and confinement for thirty days on bread and water. Guards, remove this man from my court.

"Corporal Brewer, you likewise have been found guilty. You are hereby sentenced to be branded on the forehead with the letter 't' so that all may know that you are a thief. You will also receive fifty strokes of the lash and will be imprisoned until the end of the war when, at that time you will be dishonorably discharged from the United States Army."

The third and final man to be sentenced was an Irish Immigrant by the name of Tommy O'Donnell. Colonel Harney looked at the man with pure hatred in his eyes. "You Private O'Donnell, will be executed by a firing squad selected from your own company. May God have mercy on your soul for I shall have none."

A deep silence settled over the court room. The unevenness of the sentence was a great shock to all. "The Judge Advocate will finalize the verdict and submit it to the Commanding General for approval. Court is adjourned."

The Rangers left the court room and were returning to the company area when Wally asked: "Sam, why the uneven sentencing? All three are equally guilty. Why not the same ruling?"

"But Wally, one was much more guilty in the eyes of the court." Sam replied to Wally's question.

"Explain that to me." Wally was searching for an answer." How can O'Donnell be guilty more than the others?"

"It's simple; the first two men are native born Americans. O'Donnell is Irish born and not even a citizen of America."

"The Verdict wasn't fair!" Wally spoke angrily.

"Of all the words to describe Colonel Harney, fair is not one of them." Sam said seriously.

Colonel Bliss was disturbed by the verdict. "General Scott, I must protest this verdict! Colonel Harney has once again demonstrated his bias. I implore you to set it aside."

"No, Colonel Bliss, I will not! We must make an example of these men. Discipline must be maintained. Sign the order for execution and forward it to the man's

Commanding Officer!" With a heavy heart Colonel Bliss did as he was ordered. Colonel Bliss loved the Army. It was his life but at times he was deeply saddened at the unfairness of certain officers.

TWENTY-SIX

Just before sunset the convicted man was led to the execution grounds. The stables had a high fence and the man O'Donnell was tied to the upright. The Archbishop stood with the man hearing his last confession and performing last rites. When the Archbishop moved away the Officer in Charge of the firing detail approached the unfortunate man and offered him a blind ford which he refused. "Any last words?" he asked. The Officer returned to the rifle squad and began the drill "Ready, Aim, Fire!" Just as the rifles barked O'Donnell shouted, "Aim straight boys!"

The execution of the Irish soldier cast a shadow over the camp. Nativist celebrated his death while the Irish and others seethed over the unfair treatment. Many others resented the mutilation of the offenders. None were of the opinion that they didn't need to be punished but all agreed it was unfair to punish one more than the other. Resentment filled the Immigrants hearts.

Several days after the unjust execution another incident occurred that would have dire consequences. Desertions were occurring at a rapid rate and most were Irish with several other nationalities also going over the hill. Colonel Harney had in his command an Irishman who curried favor with the Colonel. He informed Harney of a Mexican Priest who was harboring seven deserters in his home. Colonel Harney decided to do something about the matter. He set a watch on the house of the Catholic Priest, one Padre Rafael Ignacio Cortez. That very day an American soldier slipped into the garden of the house. The traitor raced to report to Colonel Harney.

Colonel Harney assembled a squad of his elite cavalrymen, Nativists all and rode to the Father's residence.

He ordered a big cavalryman to kick down the door without knocking first and the men rushed in to find the Catholic Priest kneeling in front of a small alter.

"Where are my men?" Harney demanded. He reached down and grasped the Father's robes and yanked him to his feet. "I repeat you bastard, where are the men?"

The Catholic priest was speechless. He believed that his home was above search. The Government would not have allowed a search of the house. When he failed to answer Harney threw him aside. "Search the place!" He ordered.

The Cavalrymen did a cursory search and found nothing. "Search again!" Harney ordered.

A young soldier was searching the pantry just off the kitchen when he noticed scuff marks on the floor. He motioned for his Sergeant and pointed to the marks. As a rifleman stood aiming at the wall they slid the barrier away. Inside they found seven American Soldiers who had deserted their Army.

The men were herded in front of Colonel Harney. "Bind and rope them and deliver them to the Provost Marshall."

The men were roped together and led from the house. Colonel Harney grasped the Catholic clergyman and thrust him out the door. "Him too!" He ordered.

"Colonel, this man is a civilian! A priest no less. I'm not sure we've the authority to arrest him." One of the Cavalrymen said.

"Arrest him on my authority. I am declaring Martial Law." The Colonel said.

The prisoners were delivered to the Provost to await trial. Colonel Harney drew up Court Martial papers charging the seven deserters and then considered bringing charges against the Catholic priest. He sought guidance from Colonel Bliss.

"Colonel Harney, declaring Martial law is a serious matter and is not in your control. Only General Scott as the Commanding General can declare Martial Law." Colonel Bliss advised Colonel Harney.

"Harney, why did you try to declare Martial Law?" General Scott asked.

"So I could try that papist priest for inciting the troops to revolt and concealing them so they could desert." Colonel Harney said angrily.

"What I would like you to do is drop any charges against these men and release the Priest." General Scott asked.

"No General, it is the right of any American officer to prefer charges against offenders. I insist on a Court Martial!" Colonel Harney said.

"Very well, fill out the charges and file them with the Judge Advocate's Office. You're dismissed!" General Scott left no doubt he wished Harney gone from his sight.

"General Scott, I doubt we have the authority to try a civilian in front of a Military Court. The Articles of War do not apply unless Martial Law is declared." Perfect Bliss said.

"You're correct in that. But there is more than one way to skin a polecat. Please ask Major Lee to see me." General Scott had trained as a lawyer before becoming an officer in the Army.

"Major Lee reporting as ordered."

"William, will you leave us alone for a moment?" General Scott asked his Adjutant.

"Major Lee, you're my best officer. Stern but fair in all you're dealings with the enlisted men. I must swear you to secrecy in this matter." Scott explained Colonel Harney's entrapment of the deserters and his arrest of the Priest.

"General it has been time since I studied the Articles back at the Point but I'm sure there is no way to try the Priest and as to the supposed deserters I couldn't convict them in good conscious."

"I'm not asking that you do, as a matter of fact I think the parties to the Court Martial should all be acquitted." General Scott replied.

"What are you suggesting General?" Lee asked.

"I shall appoint you President of the Court and appoint officers with no 'nativist' view for the members of the Court.

Zealous B. Tower will handle the Defense. You'll be free to vote on the case as you see fit. The only unorthodox thing about the trial will be the Priest's role. He must be acquitted!" General Scott said. "Do you understand?"

"Perfectly, General. When do we convene the court?" Lee asked.

"After Lunch tomorrow." Please ask Colonel Bliss to step in."

"Colonel Bliss, I should like you to cut orders forming a Courts-Martial Board. Major Robert E. Lee will be presiding officer. Zealous B. Tower is appointed Defense Council and assign U.S. Grant, P.T. Beauregard, Mick Malone and two other officers to the Board. The Trial is to convene tomorrow afternoon."

"Yes sir!" Colonel Bliss said smiling. The old man had found a way around the difficult position that Harney had placed him in. Taps was sounding over the city calling all soldiers to rest as the Colonel finished the charging documents.

The new day dawned bright and clear. The Mexican sun began to warm the city and the fragrance of all manner of blooming flowers drifted on the slight breeze. Sam and Wally went to the grand dining room where Colonel Hays sat enjoying his morning coffee. "I could get used to this." He swept his hand of the room. It wasn't just grand, it was eloquent. "What are you boys up to today?" Colonel Hays asked.

"We are going to the square and have breakfast at the open air café. Then we'll visit the Musee until lunch and after that we'll attend the trial."

"I've no use for the Museum but I'll attend that trial. I want to see how the Old Man pulls it off." Hays replied.

"What do you mean?" Sam asked.

"I bet all the defendants are acquitted. Harney exceeded his authority and gave the Command a black eye. Now Old Fuss and Feathers has to fix the matter. An acquittal does that admirably. Then the entire mess goes away." Colonel Hays explained.

TWENTY-SEVEN

After lunch Sam and Wally found places near the front of the court room and listened to the charging document being read. The last name on the list was Father Cortez's name. The charge was harboring the deserters.

"A moment!" Major Lee said. "Who charged this man?"

"I did!" Colonel Harney shouted.

"Colonel, this man is a civilian and as such is not subject to this court unless Martial law is declared. You're aware of that?" Major Lee asked.

"But I did declare Martial Law!" Harney shouted.

"That was an error on your part. Only the Commanding General, General Scott can declare that." Major Lee said softly.

A deep red blush of anger rose up on Harney's face and he jumped to his feet. He was about to say something when Major Lee ordered him to sit down. Unsure of what to do he obeyed the order and sat down.

"Father Cortez, the court apologizes for any inconvenience this matter may have caused you. You are free to go."

A wide smile appeared on Colonel Hay's face which was a rare thing. "I told you so." He whispered to Sam.

The trial wound down and the sentencing phase began. "Prisoners will rise and face the court." Major Lee ordered. "All defendants are found guilty of being absent without leave and are sentenced to ten days in confinement on bread and water and one half a month's pay."

General Scott smiled when he received the verdict. "William, execute the verdict and when these men are released from confinement see that they are assigned to other units. I don't want them anywhere near Harney."

Many immigrants heard of the verdict and were in awe, especially the Irish Catholics. Desertions dropped off for a while. Colonel Harney increased his unfair punishment of the Irish and German Catholics for even the most minor offense and for many imagined offenses as well. Soon the number of desertions doubled.

"You'd think the stupid bastards would learn!" Wally said. "The more they mistreat those Irish, the more of them go over the hill."

"Yeah', Sam agreed, 'can't really blame them though, they're taught that shit at West Point and writers like that O'Sullivan feed the flames. It's the religious thing. Catholic's are not the same and, frankly, I find their faith very mysterious."

"But you don't hate them?" Wally questioned.

"Way I see it, everyman is free to believe what he wishes.' Sam said, 'It's a God given right!"

"Oh, we'll win the war, of that I've no doubt. And Polk will get his 'manifest destiny' but I'm afraid we'll lose the peace." Wally said thoughtfully.

"How so?" Sam asked.

"The real question is not immigration but slavery. Polk is sure to take much of Mexico's lands and those will become states in time. The North is afraid that slavery will be legal in the new territories and will throw the balance of power to the south."

"That may be true but, first, we have to win this war. We've been ordered to march to the capitol where that rascal Santa Anna awaits with an army five times our size." Sam Walker informed his Sergeant.

"When do we leave for Mexico?" Wally asked.

"In the morning." Sam replied.

TWENTY-EIGHT

The American Army began the march to Puebla as the Mexican spring gave way to summer. They reach that town in the last days of May 18 1847 and set up camp. General Scott then threw the dice and did as the Conquistador Hernando Cortez had when he burned his ships in the conquest. He ordered that all his troops assemble on Puebla leaving his route of supply open and unprotected. It was a gamble!

General Santa Anna groaned when he received the news. He had neither the men nor the money to exploit this opening in Scott's rear. He concentrated on strengthening his defenses. He ordered the Saint Patrick's to man an abandoned Convent, Santa Maria de los Angeles at the town of Churubosco. The town's name meant the 'place of the War God' in Aztec. It had eight foot walls and a charming courtyard that Reilly and the other deserters quickly turned into field emplacements for the heavy cannon. Gunners piled powder and shot behind the guns and led the livestock to a safe spot behind the Convent. Reilly was as prepared as he could make the position. A Battalion of Infantry was put in place to protect the guns.

Further to the north at the town of Puebla an American Sergeant witnessed a tall blonde civilian talking to German immigrant troops and passing out broadsides to these same troops. He arrested the man and took him in front of the 'Council of War' a tribunal established by Scott to try all offenders, military and civilian. Scott had declared Martial Law and the court was empowered to try civilians.

The tall blonde civilian proved to be a German Watchmaker named Martin Tritschler who was a naturalized

Mexican citizen. He had been soliciting his countrymen to desert and join the Mexican Army and Santa Anna. Having established the right to try a civilian the case was submitted to the court. The trial which would take three days began in early June.

Martin Tritschler arrogantly faced the court. He had shown disdain for the court and had stated it was an unjust tribunal with no authority to try him. The judges disagreed.

"You have been found guilty of serious offenses including sedition and treason and this court sentences you to death by firing squad. You will be returned to custody pending review of your case by the Commanding General."

The arrogant German Watchmaker was led away to await his fate.

Colonel William 'perfect' Bliss received the Courts-Martial records and had just finished reviewing them and passed them to General Scott for his review. "There are some questions I have over this entire case." Bliss told his father-in-law. "I'm not sure we can try a foreign national for treason or sedition."

"I see no problem with the verdict. Order the Execution of Sentence!" General Scott said.

It was in the evening hours when the tall, blonde German prisoner, his hands bound behind him, was led from his cell. A Mexican priest accompanied his to the spot before a wall where a rifle squad awaited. The Priest gave the German last rites and moved away. The Officer in charge of the firing squad advanced to the unfortunate German and offered his a chance to say his last words.

"Viva la Mexico!" The German watchmaker shouted.

A blindfold was offered and disdainfully refused. The Officer moved to his position and gave the order, 'Ready, Aim, Fire'. Shots rang out in the courtyard and the German Watchmaker slumped over dead. The surgeon pronounced and the Catholic priest accompanied by townspeople recovered the body. They would lay him out in the Church for three days but the American Army would be gone before the martyr was laid to rest.

Far North in Washington an irate President James K. Polk who was fighting for a second term received the news from Mexico that Santa Anna had refused the offer he had dispatched with Mister Nickolas Twist. Santa Anna had slipped word to the President that he would seek an end to hostilities between their countries for the sum of one million dollars. Polk had sent Twist with a down payment of ten-thousand dollars to the Mexican General.

Santa Anna had taken the money and refused to see Mister Twist. He refused to return the money and continued preparation for the defense of Mexico. Diplomat Twist rode north to report to General Scott.

Commanding General Scott, The supreme Commander of all American Forces was shocked when the State Department's Minister at Large delivered the news. He had not been consulted about the matter and was amazed that Polk had made the offer behind his back. He angrily dispatched a courier to the opposition party in Congress concerning the matter.

The Whig party in Congress leaked the entire matter to the press and that would propel General Taylor into the White House. Scott was furious when he found out about the politics that would cost him the nomination. Meanwhile he had battles to plan. He summoned Major Lee and Colonel Hays to his tent.

"We need better intelligence concerning Santa Anna's troop dispositions and routes into the city. I would like each of you to select men to creep up on the city and bring back information that will help us breach the defenses." Scott asked.

"Captain Walker can scout out the left flank in front and come up with a plan to cross the Rio Churubosco and take the bridge and hold it until my Rangers and the infantry can relieve them. We will have the enemy rear and can completely encircle them. We cut the National Highway so they can't reinforce or resupply the convent." Colonel Hays suggested.

"That will leave me free to send Lieutenant Zealous Tower to the east of the Convent and find a way to come up on the enemy's rear." Major Lee suggested.

"It's a fine idea. Get me the information!" General Scott ordered. "I have to avoid the deserter's fire from that convent. Rushing down the National Road headlong into those guns would be suicide."

Sam selected Wally and two other Rangers and departed on his mission. They gained the bridge and brought back one terrified Mexican Soldier who had strayed from his post. General Scott was greatly pleased. "You have good news for me, Captain Wilson?"

"Yes Sir, we found a way to the bridge over the Rio Churubosco and actually gained the abutment under the bridge using an old Comanche Indian trick. We cut hollow reeds and stayed under the water until we were under the bridge deck. On the way back we captured this man who had left his post to relieve himself. Wally cut a few more reeds to show his troops how to use them." Sam reported.

"How will it work exactly?" Scott asked.

"My Rangers and I will infiltrate the bridge and remain hidden several hours in advance of the actual attach. Then, when the rest of the Rangers and your Infantry begin to charge the bridge, we'll rush out from under the bridge and make short work of them." Sam explained.

"You're sure you can take the bridge with no problems?" General Scott asked.

Sam removed one of his Colt 44's and handed it to the General. Each Ranger carries two of these pistols and can fire 10 rounds before the Mexican Infantry can get off one shot with their muzzle loading Brown Bess muskets. Then after he's fired that shot he has to reload. We will have fired 10 or 15 rounds by that time and all those not killed will either run or surrender."

Major Robert E. Lee examined the weapon when Scott handed it back. He surveyed it with an Engineer's eye and was impressed by what he had seen. "I shall petition the War Department to purchase the revolvers for my men!" He said.

It was an hour later when Lieutenant Tower reported to his CO. "The frontal assault would be suicide! The road runs downhill for five hundred yards and then it dips slightly lower. The guns would be safe enough but the Infantry will be cut to pieces." Tower paused. "Further to the east lies an ancient lave field that the Mexicans think is impassable. I believe that a road, wide enough for artillery, could be cut through that tangled mess. The sounds of the chopping would alert the Mexicans on the bluff."

"The Mexicans have fortified the bluffs overlooking the Pedregal? "Scott asked.

"General Valencia informed Santa Anna that he could protect the National Road better from the high ground and that the 'impassable' lava field would prevent an attack from that direction." Lieutenant Tower said.

"Good work, Lieutenant. Now go get some rest. I shall need you tomorrow." General Scott dismissed the young West Pointer.

"Major Lee, How do you feel about cutting that dam road through the lave fields?" General Scott asked.

"I don't have enough men to accomplish that." Lee replied.

"Then perhaps General Pillow will be kind enough to lend you a company or two of his men. Could you accomplish it then?" Scott asked.

"Sir, if Lieutenant Tower says that it can be done, we will do it." Lee replied.

TWENTY-NINE

The heavy rains began to drench the field before Lee and his men marched to the southern edge of the lava fields. The rain chilled the men and made the work more difficult. Some shots were heard coming from the bluff and work ceased until it was determined that they were fired at some other target. The heavy downpour drove the Mexican sentries back to the shelter of their camp leaving the bluff unattended. General Valencia declared a great victory and returned to his tent where he proceeded to get drunk. Many of his soldiers joined him and there was no one to hear the sounds that issued from the lava field. Work went on throughout the night and before dawn the road through the Pedregal was complete.

Three cannon were being manually hauled over the makeshift trail with the help of a young West Pointer. Major Lee recognized the officer. It was Lieutenant Grant, the Quartermaster.

"Sam, what are you doing up here with the troops?" Major Lee asked.

"Things are pretty slow at the Quartermaster department. I thought I'd like to see some action and make myself useful." Sam Grant explained.

"Very well!' Lee answered. 'Let's get those guns into battery." Major Lee laid a hand to the emplacement of the cannon.

The rains had stopped falling and the bright Mexican sun was just peeking over the horizon as the Americans took up position behind large chunks of lava. "Lieutenant Grant, how well do you remember your lessons in artillery maneuvers from your time at the Point?"

"They are still fresh in my mind, Sir." Sam Grant replied.

"In that case I'm placing you in temporary command of these guns. The ridgeline up there will be your first target but do not fire until the command is given." Major Lee went to see to the other parts of his line.

Far over on the left flank two dozen Texas Rangers picketed their horses and slipped into the waters of the Rio Churubosco and began to inch up stream. A threat of their discovery only occurred once before they reached the bridge. They used the hollow reeds to submerge beneath the waters and when the Mexicans moved away they continued their journey. Long before the new day dawned they were safely hidden beneath the bridge deck.

Above the bridge, at the convent, the Irish soldiers of Mexico waited for the light blue line of American Infantry to appear on the road. They had eaten their morning meal and had assumed their posts to await the attack they knew was coming in their direction. Each man knew that they had to win this battle or face the hangman's noose. The Mexican Infantry guarding the guns felt no such urgency. If they lost they would be taken prisoner and treated fairly by the Americans.

Colonel Morales waited with Reilly and the San Patricio's for the initial onslaught of the American army. He knew that if the Convent was lost then Mexico would lose the war and so he wished to remain with his troops. A messenger arrived with a massage from General Santa Anna. Morales read it and frowned.

"John,' Colonel Morales said, 'I've been ordered to report to General Santa Anna. You're in command here. Maintain this position! If the Convent falls so does Mexico!"

Reilly Saluted and said: "We shall do our best!"

With a heavy heart, Colonel Morales spurred his mount for the city and Santa Anna's HQ. He knew that the Saint Patrick Battalion would give its all considering the fate that awaited them should they lose. He worried about the Infantry assigned to protect his guns. Many were conscripts who had no stake in the outcome.

The battle for Churubosco began with one round of artillery fired from defilade on the road where it dipped out of sight. It struck one of John's guns killing the entire crew and rendering the cannon useless.

A nervous San Patricio gunner returned the shot.

"Hold your fire! Wait for the Infantry to appear." John Reilly snapped. "Fire only on my command."

Time seemed to stand still with every second seeming like an hour and every minute like a day. The Americans hidden by the crest in the road waited before beginning the attack. John Reilly went from gun to gun offering encouragement and checking its status. Finally the powder blue uniforms of the American Infantry appeared on the road. "Fire" John barked. The thin blue line staggered and came on. Only several hundred yards separated the two armies.

Far from the Convent the remainder of the Ranger Companies and two flights of the 2nd Dragoons charged the bridge. Sam and his little band or Rangers rushed up the embankment and took the bridge. Those Mexicans who hadn't fled at the first shot threw up their hands and surrendered. The entire battle for the bridge over the Rio Churubosco lasted only a few moments and the enemy rear was open to the American advance.

Sam and his Rangers regained their mounts and joined the others in an encircling movement of the Convent.

At the Pedregal the action was getting heavy. The Mexicans had regained the ridge and were pouring fire onto the Americans. General Valencia had sent an Infantry column down a trail to the road and they engaged to Infantry of Pillows division in hand to hand combat. The fight ebbed and flowed for some time until Sam Grant horsed one of the runs onto the road and laid down a tremendous fire on the Mexican troops who edged their way up the hill and ran for the city. No officer remained on the bluff to rally the troops.

General Valencia had escaped the area and was well on his way to Mexico City.

Sam Grant and his cannon had cleared the bluff of cannon and infantry. The National Road was in American hands. Troops had been ordered to the bluff and General Valencia's former position. They found the camp undisturbed. It was as the Mexican Forces had left it in their hurry to escape the Americans.

The National Road was in American hands and no reinforcement or supplies could reach the city. The only way out was to the west. Santa Anna and his staff were preparing to leave the troubled city.

Sam Walker and his Rangers together with a party of the 2nd Dragoon had reached the rear of the Convent encountering only light resistance. They rested a moment while the assault on the edifice at the front of the building continued.

THIRTY

John Reilly glumly assessed the situation. It would be over soon since his cannon had been destroyed one by one until only a single remained cannon remained in service. It was down to the last rounds when a lucky hit destroyed that gun also.

"Everyone withdraw inside the Convent!" John ordered.

A Mexican officer tried to run up the white flag of surrender when John and his men discovered this. He angrily tore the white banner down. On two more occasions Mexicans attempted to run up the flag of surrender. Twice more the Saint Patrick's ripped the white flag from its pole.

The men of Pillow's force noticed that the cannon fire had ceased and so they brought their guns closer and began demolishing the front of the Convent with round shot. One shot took a ten foot piece of the front wall out. Sky blue clad American Infantry rushed through the gap in the wall. The sight that met their eyes was horrible indeed. Mexican Infantry who had not escaped the last moments of battle threw up their hands. The few Irishmen were propped up against the walls. The dead were covering the floor. The cost had been very great.

John Reilly held a dying Irishman in his arms. Both of the man's legs had been severed above the knees and there was no hope of saving him. John was trying to make his last day on earth easier.

An Infantryman raised his bayonet to skewer John Reilly when a voice hollered "Stop" It was the Ranger, Sam Walker. "Leave him be. Can't you see he is comforting one of his dying men?" Sam said.

"But, Sir. He's one of the Irish deserters who manned the guns against our men!" The rifleman said.

"Every man deserves a dignified death. You will guard this man and see that none touches him and when it is over you will conduct him to the Provost Martial where he'll meet his fate."

The soldier waited until the wounded man gasped his last and John had closed the man's eyes. John stood and told the soldier: "I'm ready to go." He was conducted to the estate where General Winfred Scott had established his HQ."

"You're John Reilly of the Saint Patrick's formerly of the United States Army?" General Scott asked of Reilly.

"I am MAJOR John Reilly of the Saint Patrick's Battalion." John replied somewhat arrogantly.

"Colonel Bliss, contact the Provost and have him turn those stables into a prison where he will hold these deserters for Courts-Martial. Prepare the charging documents. They charges will be desertion and going over to the enemy and firing on American Troops."

John was conducted to the stables that now served as his prison. Many of his former companions awaited him. "How many are we?" John asked.

"You make thirty five. What's to become of us?" One of the Irish deserters asked.

"It's quite simple. General Scott will convene a Court Martial and we will be tried and found guilty and then we'll be hanged." John told the man.

The man shuddered and said nothing.

General Scott had summoned Major Robert E. Lee to his Headquarters. He had a difficult mission for the best man in his command.

"Robert,' General Scott began, 'I would like you to defend the Irish deserters. We both know that they will be found guilty and hanged. Their offenses are particularly heinous and every man in the Army wants their blood. If you can find any mitigating circumstances please introduce them. It gives me no pleasure sending such valiant soldiers to their death. Will you do it for me?"

"I find the whole matter distasteful but I shall do my best." Major Lee agreed to take the job.

"I've ordered that you be given unfettered access to the accused. I realize how difficult this will be for you but you're the only man I can trust with the Job." Scott stated.

Major Lee went to meet his charges. He found a tough group of Irishmen largely resigned to their fate. He explained the proceeding would begin in the morning and offered little hope for the outcome. He wrote down each man's name, rank and date of desertion. None of the men could offer anything new to the situation.

"I'll do what I can but the outlook is bleak." Lee said.

"Sir,' Reilly said, 'this man is an idiot and I believe he should not be tried because he's quite obviously insane."

"That would certainly be a viable defense in his case. I shall consult General Scott in his case. Perhaps he may be spared the hangman's noose." Major Lee left the men and returned to Scott. He explained the idiot soldier's inability to understand what was happening to him.

"I think the charges against this man must stand. If he is convicted and sentenced to hang I will mitigate his sentence upon review." General Scott said. "One out of thirty five is not good but it is something."

"I have a list here of all the men and the dates of their desertions." He handed the list to the Adjutant. Lee saluted and left. He had much to do before the court convened.

THIRTY-ONE

The next morning the court convened in the great hall of the residence that Scott had chosen for the trial. The court consisted of Colonel Bennett Riley, Captain Braxton Bragg, Lieutenant Zealous B. Tower, Lieutenant Mick Malone and Lieutenant U. S. Grant as members of the Court. Colonel Harney acted as the prosecution.

The charging documents were read and each man's name was read into the record. The accused men would be given the chance to call witnesses favorable to them. The first was John's former Company Commander.

"State you name and rank and your connection to this case." Colonel Riley ordered.

"My Name is Moses Emory Merrill, Major. At the time I commanded Company 'K' of the fifth Infantry. The man John Reilly was under my command."

"What sort of soldier was the defendant, a slacker, no doubt." Colonel Harney suggested.

"On the contrary!" Major Merrill said. "I found him to be an excellent soldier and never had to punish him. He performed better than most probably because of his former service in the British Army."

"Would you tell the court the circumstances concerning his desertion?" Colonel Harney asked.

"On Sunday the 12th of April he came to me to request a pass to attend Catholic service at a civilian home. Since he was a model soldier I gave him the pass and have not seen or heard of him again until now."

Major Lee approached the Major and asked: "You say you never punished the defendant?"

"No, never." Major Merrill stated.

"To your knowledge was he punished by other officers in your command?" Lee asked.

"There was one incident that occurred with Captain Braxton Bragg. Riley was forced to be bucked and gagged for some offense. I told Bragg to bring any such matters to me and I would decide if the matter warranted punishment. That is the correct way to handle these matters."

"What offense did Bragg cite as cause for punishment?" Major Lee asked.

"Captain Bragg said that Reilly failed to salute properly." Merrill answered.

"Yet you didn't believe him?" Lee asked. "Why not?"

"Because when he joined my company he saluted in the British Army manner and I had to instruct him in the way we Americans performed it."

The trial continued most of the day and it was late in the afternoon when the board returned to pronounce sentence.

"Defendants will rise and face the court!" Colonel Bennett Riley ordered.

"All of the defendants are found guilty of desertion and are sentenced to hang pending review by the Commanding General." Colonel Riley and the officers of the Court left the courtroom.

General Scott hung his head low as he read the Court-Martial findings. He handed the papers to Colonel Bliss. "Thirty five men. Scott said.

Major Robert E. Lee arrived at General Scott's Headquarters requesting an interview. He had been the Defense Council for the convicted deserters.

"Major Lee, what is it you wanted?" Scott asked.

"General, I've been reading the Articles of War and I believe a terrible mistake has been made."

"What mistake, Major?" Scott asked.

"Well sir, according to Article Twelve, a man convicted of desertion can only be executed in time of war. These eight deserted before the war began." Lee pointed to his list. "It would not be legal to hang those eight."

Colonel Bliss consulted a copy of the Articles. "I'm afraid he's correct in that, General." He offered the Articles of war to the General.

"Well, they still have to be punished. What do you recommend?" General Scott asked.

"The Court will have to reconvene and a different sentence imposed." Bliss stated.

"There is one other thing, this ninth man is an idiot. He doesn't know right from and I believe him to be insane. It would not be right to sentence him with his disability. Perhaps you could soften his sentence?"

"Call the Court back into session. I want this done with. Tomorrow the Marines and the Fifth Infantry begin the assault on Chapultepec Castle and I wish this matter concluded by the time they take that fortress."

The Court returned to deliberating the nine men's sentence. The Nativist officers wanted the strongest terms allowed. The others balked.

A sentence that was grudgingly accepted was forwarded to Scott. He read the paper and turned to Colonel Bliss. Appoint Colonel Harney as executioner but tell him not to hang the culprits until Old Glory is raised on Chapultepec Castle."

Colonel Bliss conveyed these instructions to Colonel Harney who sourly accepted them. He had insisted that all the deserters hang. Hadn't they all fired on his men?

Lieutenant Gillispie and his Marines were attacking the grounds before the Castle. They were making good progress and had captured most of the artillery and over run the Infantry arrayed outside the Castle. Lieutenant Mick Malone and his men were also making gains. The Castle must fall soon. He was unaware that until they captured the edifice the Irishmen would live. Many of those same clung to a desperate hope that they would be rescued at the last moment from the gibbet. Others wished it was over.

It was nearing nightfall and the Castle had still not fallen into American hands. Gillispie and his Marines and the soldiers of the 5th settled in for a long night. As the shadows lengthened and the dark began to close over the field, one of the Marines found a dead Mexican. He was dressed in a gaudy uniform unlike any that the Marine had seen before.

"Sir, Look at this!" He pointed to the dead Mexican.

The lieutenant approached the body. "What about it?" He asked.

"He's only a kid!" The Marine said. "Probably about 14 or 15. Is Santa Anna that desperate?"

"He is probably an underclassman." The lieutenant said.

Noticing the puzzled look on the Marine's face he continued. 'This Castle is the home of the Mexican Military Academy, something like our West Point. He is one of the Cadets that they armed and put to the defense of this edifice."

"Lieutenant I don't like the idea of killing kids." The Marine said.

"Nor I." Lieutenant Gillispie said. "Get used to it because there a lot more defending Chapultepec. I think the entire Cadet Corps turned out against us."

"It just doesn't seem fair." The Marine said.

"Well if they fight as courageously as they have so far we'll have a bad day tomorrow. Better get some rest." Gillispie moved off on his rounds checking on his Marines. The night would be very long as the Marines anticipated the morning's action.

"Sir,' the Marine asked 'this place they call Chapultepec hill, what does that mean?"

"It translates to Hill of the grasshoppers, Grasshopper Hill." Gillispie informed the Marine.

"Mexico is a very strange place!" The Marine said.

THIRTY-TWO

Reveille sounded over the American encampment. The prisoners had been fed and Colonel Harney had formed his troops on parade. The prisoners were led out into the open space and drawn up in formation.

Nine men were led to the fence and secured to fence posts. A burly Mexican mule skinner stood at each post. Nine cat 'o nine tail flogs were distributed among the Mexicans. Colonel Harney had insisted that the Mexicans do the flogging that his men would not sully their hand with the distasteful chore. Privately a few believed he used the Mexicans because they would not spare the whip. The Colonel drew his horse up facing the prisoners and read the sentence. General Order 283, Army of Occupation specified the sentence.

"The following named men will be taken from their place of confinement and conducted to the place of execution where they shall receive 50 lashes, well laid on the bare back. Then they shall be branded on the right cheek with the letter 'D' so that all may know they are deserters. Then they shall be confined at hard labor until the Army leaves Mexico. Signed; General Winfred Scott, Commanding. According to General Order 320 of the Army of Occupation let the punishment begin."

A long drum roll sounded through the yard and when it stopped Harney screamed "Execute!"

Mexican mule skinners raised their flogs and as Colonel Harney counted they began to lay on the lash. The Idiot was the first to cry out. John Reilly bit his lip and kept silent. Another man screamed in pain. The beatings continued until the count reached fifty.

Colonel Harney prodded his to the spot where John Reilly was fettered. "One more lash!" He instructed the Mexicans. As the 51st stroke fell on his back John passed out. The Surgeon came forward with his orderlies and began smearing salt into the wounded men's backs.

"Halt!' Colonel Harney said. "Revive them first!"

A look of pure hatred passed over the Surgeon's face as he stepped aside and allowed an orderly to rouse the Irish Prisoners.

"You May begin." Harney said.

When all nine backs had been administered to the deserters were arraigned to one side with a view of the gallows. The quartermaster had provided wagons and the guards forced the convicts sentenced to stand in the wagons and forced a noose over the convicted man's head. They waited for something to happened but the Mexicans who had been assigned to each wagon were off to one side.

John and his eight companions waited as the Mexican Muleteers heated cattle brands in the fire. When they were cherry red Colonel Harney rode by each man as the branding iron was applied. Men screamed in pain. When John's time came the Mexican applied the brand to his left cheek.

"No! You stupid bastard. The right cheek. Apply the brand to the right cheek!" Harney had noticed that the Mexican had been about to brand the wrong cheek but had said nothing. John fainted from the searing pain. The Surgeon applied the salt to the unconscious Reilly as Harney was looking away. John became aware that he'd been branded twice. He hated Harney.

"What are they waiting for?" One of the others asked.

"The worst is over for us but I think they wish us to see our friends hang." John said.

"God but that salt in the wounds hurt." Patrick said. He was still feeling the pain.

"It was done for a good cause." John Reilly replied. "Without the salt the wounds turn septic and there is no cure for that."

"How long do we have to wait?" One of the men asked.

"Keep your eyes on yon Castle for I've a hunch when it falls the horses will be whipped forward sending our men to hell." John said.

Colonel Harney had noticed something amiss. "Where is the 26th man?" He demanded to know.

The Surgeon came forward to report. "He's in the hospital. He had both legs blown off and he is almost dead."

"Drag the rascal out and place him in his noose. I've orders to hang twenty six and by God twenty six I will hang!" Harney shouted.

Several orderlies went to the hospital and fetched the wounded man. The Quartermaster provided a wooden barrel to prop the man on and he was hoisted into position. He died as the noose was affixed to his neck and one of the orderlies began to unfasten it.

"What are you doing?" Colonel Harney bellowed.

"The man is dead. There's no use hanging him now." The orderly answered.

"Leave him!" Harney ordered. "I shall hang twenty six this day."

At the Castle the Marines charged the gate and gained entrance, the others followed and hand to hand combat broke out. The Americans captured the first floor and then rushed to the second. They were opposed be the cadets more than regulars and the victory was only moments away. All of the Cadets were struck down and only three managed to gain entrance to the Commandant's Office. The Americans were battering down the door and almost succeeded when the three Cadets wrapped themselves in the Mexican Colors and leaped from the parapet to their deaths far below. A sudden silence fell over the troops. All firing ceased and those closest to the spot where the cadet had jumped gaped at their sacrifice.

Lieutenant Gillispie tore down the Mexican flag and ran up Old Glory. It was over.

"Execute!" Harney bellowed as Mexican muleteers flogged their charges and twenty six bodies swung at the end of their ropes. Many of the prisoners struggled for some moments before they went limp. The Legion of Strangers was no more and the Country for which they had shed their blood was in American hands.

Two wagons led by Catholic Priests entered the square in front of Scotts Headquarters and began to collect their honored dead.

Colonel Harney rushed forward and stopped the Priests. General Scott noticed the disturbance and approached Colonel Harney. "What is happening, Colonel?" Scott asked.

"General, these filthy papist priests are collecting the bodies for burial. They should be buried in pauper's field and their graves left unmarked."

"No Colonel, they belong to Mexico now. They fought bravely on her behalf and deserve to be honored by the Mexicans. You will allow the Catholic Priests to claim the bodies." General Scott found a perverse pleasure in thwarting Colonel Harney's plan.

Colonel Harney huffed but stood aside to allow the clerics to gather the dead San Patricio's bodies. When they completed their collection of the dead and began to leave General Scott rendered a hand salute.

THIRTY-THREE

The date was September 10th. On the 11th a few more San Patricio soldiers were executed at Mixoc prison. The Irish Catholics of Mexico ceased to exist. The war degenerated to small skirmishes with bands of soldier that roamed free.

The Mexican Priests bore the dead Irishman to a field directly in front of the Convento of Santa Maria de Los Angeles where they had fought their last battle. The Priests knew no names for the Irishmen and so they were buried with one simple marker. "Here lies the soldiers of the Heroic Saint Patrick's Battalion who gave their lives for Mexico. May they rest in final peace." No Flags, bugles or rifle squad marked the occasion. Only the Catholic priest would remember where their last remains were placed.

An emissary from President Polk arrived in Scott's Headquarters and the end of the month. It was Nickolas Twist of the State Department and he brought papers empowering him to negotiate the peace with the Mexican Government.

Santa Anna had fled Mexico for the island nation of Cuba under the Spanish Flag. He requested asylum and was granted it by the Spanish Governor. He would spend his days awaiting the call from his beloved Mexico. It never came.

The Mexican Government had fled to Guadalupe Hildago where they received the Diplomat Nicholas Twist. The members of the Government listened in horror as Twist gave them President Polk's terms They argued among themselves unable to accept the harsh conditions demanded of them.

Mister Twist repaired to his quarters and awaited their answer. Meanwhile Reilly and the other prisoners were moved to the Castle. This was caused when one of the men escaped. His wife had visited him and when she left she had another woman accompanying her. The escape was not learned of until the next day. Then they discovered that the man had left with the other 'wife'.

The haggling continued at Guadalupe Hildado for weeks. The prisoners continued to work at hard labor while the talks went on among the Mexican leaders.

"What are the terms they asked?" An elderly delegate asked one of the others.

"The Gringos want all lands north of the Rio Grande to California from a line drawn from the top edge of Texas straight across to California. Santa Fe and New Mexico and Arizona are included in that demand." The presiding officer informed the elderly man.

"That's over a half a million square miles!' He said.

"We must give up all claims to Texas too." The first man said.

They've agreed to settle all claims against Mexico and to pay 15 million's for the land in addition."

They sent for the Diplomat Mister Twist. He came smiling into their presence. "You've made up your mind to accept my Government's Offer?"

"We must first be reassured that our citizens who are left behind will be treated kindly and that they will receive American Citizenship. Their Property must be respected!"

"That is agreeable with the Government of the United States. Today is the second of February 1848. I shall finish the treaty and bring it to you for your signature."

The Mexican Priests had performed the last rites and taken the bodies to the field in front of the Convent. Mexican laborers had dug graves and the funeral services were done in the rites of the Church. A priest blessed the burial ground and they sadly turned their steps back the way they came. Only one monument graced the grave site. It read, 'here lay the heroic Irish soldiers who gave their life for Mexico'.

On three February the Treaty of Guadalupe was signed by all parties and Nickolas Twist departed for Washington where it had to be ratified by the United States Senate. They immediately accepted it. On the same day General Zachary Taylor threw his hat in the ring. He would accept the Whig nomination for president. Called the hero of Monterrey he was immensely popular with the American Public while President Polk was almost universally disliked.

A courier was dispatched for Mexico City bearing the ratified Treaty of Guadalupe, the war was over.

General Winfield Scott received the document with a sigh. He had also received the news about General Taylor accepting the nomination that he had set his heart on.

"Colonel Bliss, please begin making preparations for the Rogue's March. We shall release all those prisoners held pending the outcome of this war. Then we must plan our trip home. Please have Major Lee and the Quartermaster Grant come to see me."

The prisoners were lined up and Regular Soldiers began to shave their heads with bloody results. They were returned to their cells for the evening to await their release in the Morning.

It was nine o'clock on a chilly March day when the Saint Patrick and other prisoners were brought to the square. The troops were lined up in parade formation and the drums began to strike a tattoo as the band began the strains of the Rogue's March. The prisoners were run between the ranks of troops to the end of the square. The guard detached itself and returned to the prison. It was over!

An elegant horse drawn carriage waited not far from the point where the Irishmen were turned loose. A lovely lady stepped out and offered her hand to John. "Please, get in."

"Colonel Reilly, I am Serora Fannie Maye Calderon, my husband is a Minister of the Government. We offer you the hospitality of our home until you're ready to travel to Guadalupe Hildago." She said graciously.

"But Senora, I am a Major and not a Colonel." John informed her.

"Oh no, Senor. While you were kept in prison and Santa Anna went into exile in Cuba, the new Government voted you a promotion to Colonel. But I speak out of turn. They wish to tell you in person."

The carriage pulled through the gates of a large mansion and John was shown into a guest bedroom. It was a very large room tastefully decorated with heavy Spanish oak furniture. It was luxurious in every respect. A knock on the door and the mistress of the house entered followed by a man servant.

"Your uniform is in rags and you can't meet the President in those clothes. These were my husbands. They should fit, try them on." She turned and left the room the man servant following after her.

"Tomorrow you will ride to Guadalupe to meet the President. He has a difficult job putting this country back in order and would like your help." The woman informed Reilly.

The following morning John Reilly found a beautiful Mexican mount waiting along with a letter of introduction to President Penya e Penya and instructions for the route to Guadalupe. He mounted the horse and said goodbye.

He presented the letter to the president of Mexico and was shown into his presence.

"A pleasure to finally meet you. You and your men have served faithfully and well the cause of Mexico. Could I ask that you continue your career in the Army of Mexico?" The President asked.

"What is it you ask of me sir?" John asked.

"Since the war ended we have had uprisings in ten different states. The Army is demoralized after its defeat at the hands of the Yankees. I Offer you a full Colonelcy and the means to raise a battalion to put down these rebels."

John Reilly smiled. "I should be proud to offer my services."

"My Adjutant has your money and the deed to lands you may wish to acquire. Mexico pays its debt to our honored heroes."

John Reilly late of the Saint Patrick's Battalion saluted and rode off into history.